Easy TEFL Guide to Teaching English as a Foreign Language

T. S. Seifert

Introduction

Congratulations on taking the first step towards one of the most exciting careers in the world. You may be a university student looking for adventure, a career professional in need of change, or just looking for a way to explore the world while experiencing another culture through teaching. In any case, Teaching English as a Foreign Language (TEFL) will open up the world to anyone interested in seeing things through a different lens. You can travel the globe and earn a decent living as you teach English to students from cultures different than your own, sharing with one another a global perspective not found anywhere else. You may have young learners, adolescent students, and adult students also looking to expand their knowledge and horizons through learning English. You will form a lifelong bond with the students you meet and the cultures you will experience during your career as an English as a Foreign Language (EFL) teacher. Adventure, travel, passion, kindness, friendship, and deep understanding of a once distant place are all things you will experience as a certified TEFL teacher.

As a TEFL teacher you will have the freedom to pack your bags, leap out into the world, and discover new cultures, languages, and traditions that most will only see from a vacation resort tour bus.

TEFL teachers experience the local community and often become members of the communities they work and live in. You will have the chance to share your culture while learning another as you teach and mentor your students to success in learning a new and exciting language. You are not only teaching them a new language, but in some cases giving them a new skill set to reach their goals and fulfill their dreams. English has become a global language that is almost necessary for travel minded non-English speakers as well as career professionals located around the world. This TEFL guide will give you the essential knowledge you will need to give successful and fun EFL classes to any eager students regardless of English level, age, and interests. You will develop the key skills needed for lesson plan development, teaching important English concepts, organizing your classroom, keeping control of your material and students, as well as developing a teacher style conducive to fun academic learning.

Essential Material

Chapter One: Starting Out with Levels

What to Expect

English Language Levels and Material

The Beginner Student

The Elementary Student

The Pre-Intermediate Student

The Intermediate Student

The Advanced Student

Student Levels Concluded

Chapter Two: Keeping Lessons Relevant and Controlled

Relevant Teaching is Relevant Learning

Scaling Lesson Material

Outlining Aims and Objectives

Talking Time and Length

Chapter Three: Lesson Plan Basics

Developing a PPP Lesson Plan

Presentation Stage

Practice Stage

Production Stage

Teacher Talk Time (TTT)

Lesson Plan Format

Lesson Plan Checklist

Chapter Four: Presentation Teaching Material

Presentation Stage

Questions that Develop Answers

Creating a Visual Presentation

Showing Time as Linear

Board Work

Checking Student Competency

Chapter Five: Presentation and Vocabulary

Vocabulary Building

Vocabulary Functionality

What does it Really Mean?

Putting Words Together

Grammar Building in Presentation

Chapter Six: Practice and Organization

Use for New Vocabulary

Benefits of Practice

Presentation to Practice

Pair Practice

Group Practice

Chapter Seven: Production and Organization

Production Concepts

Production Ideas

Implementing an Exercise

Organizing Students

The New Material Trifecta

Chapter Eight: Giving Corrections and Allowing Feedback

Organizing Mistakes

Accuracy and Fluency

Body Language

Encourage Self-Correction

Student to Student Correction

Feedback Essentials

Writing Corrections

Correcting within Structure

Testing

Chapter Nine: Utilizing Coarse Materials and Textbooks

Material Outlook

The Published EFL/ESL Textbook

The Book and Student Balance

Grab Bag of Levels

Grab Bag of Ages

Text Material Structure

Creative with Lesson Material

Chapter Ten: Exceptional Classroom Management

Manage with Ownership

Organize with Precision

Psychology of Organization

Setting Rules

Maintaining Control

Handling Issues

Chapter Eleven: Reading Teaching Essentials

Is Reading Important?

The Reading Material

What's the Word?

Sentence Structure and Reading

Reading Time and Length

Chapter Twelve: Getting Into the Reading Lesson

Keep It Fun, Keep It Relevant

Ready, Set, Read

Warm Ups

Reading Comprehension

New Vocabulary

Reading Lesson Checklist

Chapter Thirteen: Writing Lesson Essentials

Why and When?

Filling the Blank Page

Developing Sentence Structure

The Paragraph

Lesson Format

Warm Ups

Warm Up Discussion

Warm Up Outline

Timing Student Writing

Chapter Fourteen: Pronunciation Development and Instruction

Pronunciation Importance

Is There an Echo in Here?

Syllable and Word Stress

Intonation Focus

Chapter Fifteen: Practical Discussion and Communication

Open Communication

Discussion Warm Ups

Communicative Activities

Keeping It Going

Expanding Conversation

When Teaching Discussion

Quality Structure

Be Engaged

Chapter Sixteen: Listening Lessons

Why Listening?

Listening Lesson Structure

Listening Lesson Material

Aspects of Listening

Chapter Seventeen: Get to Know Grammar

Grammar Basics

Nouns, Verbs, and Subjects

The Many Verb Forms

Using Prepositions

Using Articles

The Adjective Spice

Chapter One

Starting Out with Levels

Chapter Overview:

What to Expect

English Language Levels and Material

The Beginner Student

The Elementary Student

The Pre-Intermediate Student

The Intermediate Student

The Advanced Student

Student Levels Concluded

What to Expect

It's time to begin your journey as an English as a Foreign Language (EFL) teacher, first class and first day at your new profession as a qualified EFL teacher. In some ways that first lesson can be overwhelming and the butterflies in your stomach might be fluttering, but relax and know that you have the knowledge and tools necessary to be a stellar teacher. In this chapter you will hone your skills and be able to convey new English material to each one of your unique students regardless of their English level. You will find that planning a lesson, organizing class material and managing your class can be fun, insightful, and give you the confidence to build on as the school year progresses.

English Language Levels and Material

The most important factor in planning your lesson is knowing the English level of your students and their goals or specific needs with consideration to what they may already have a good comprehension of. Various academic structures or tutor schools have specific outlines that can help you craft your lesson plan, but often, especially when developing your own lesson material, you must adapt and decide what course goals you intend to cover. Knowing the basics surrounding each specific English level can aid you in adding specific grammar and vocabulary within your lesson for maximum classroom results.

In a perfect English teaching world, you would have the same students from beginning to end, Beginner to Advanced levels with all the same collective goals and interests. Unfortunately, this is almost never the case and you may have students with different goals and interests with individual knowledge of different aspects within their English level. This is the reality of EFL and as an

English teacher it is essential to develop an organic and adaptable teaching style that may help you teach effectively when you discover these issues mid-lesson. The benefit of EFL is that a student's overall general goal is the same as their classmates, regardless of level, age or profession, they all want to communicate more efficiently, express their thoughts and feelings, and have the English skill set to discuss the past, present, and future in a knowledgeable way.

Let us discuss the basics surrounding each level, including useful teaching material to think about when developing a strong, adaptable, and relevant lesson plan.

The Beginner Student

The beginner student is often regarded as the most difficult to teach based on the limited communication the teacher and student may have due to obvious language barriers. However, many teachers find this to be the most rewarding in the sense that the chance for **language discovery** is so abundant. Each new word, phrase, and grammar "ah-ha" moment is more prevalent in the beginner classroom and the sense of accomplishment can be greater for the student and teacher.

Beginner students also come in many different shapes and sizes with some students deciding to study English later in life to become more marketable in their profession. Not all beginner students are young learners and their professional backgrounds can range from doctors, lawyers, and in some cases international diplomats. It is important for you as a teacher to understand that they are professionals in their native language and may not appreciate a lesson geared for young beginners. This is where adaptability in your lesson plan comes in and knowing that your student is a beginner is not the only necessary factor when developing your lesson plan and finding material. Know your student inside and out!

Important grammar objectives useful for beginner student discovery:

The verb *to be* is an important beginner goal. Understanding its use in different forms is an essential part of the beginner's foundation. Discuss the present tense positive, negative, and question forms regarding the verb *to be*.

    ✓ **Example:** She is here (positive). She is not here (negative). Is she here (question)?

Understanding singular and plural nouns can be a fun exercise that will cause your students to not only form some important questions about the material, but also inhibit positive language discovery.

- ✓ **Example:** Book (singular), books (plural). Man vs. Men and Woman vs. Women is a great singular and plural exercise with an opportunity to add in pronunciation practice.

Question words are useful grammar tools for the beginner student and will help the student build a strong foundation for later material. We like to call them the "5Ws + H." This may help your students commit them to memory while implementing the alphabet at the same time.

- ✓ **Example:** 5Ws + H: Who, what, where, why, when, and how.

Knowing subject pronouns are important for a student to begin expressing themselves and put emphasis on the things they want to talk about or discuss in daily conversation. A lesson goal incorporating subject pronouns can also be paired with **possessive adjectives** in an interchangeable fashion.

- ✓ **Example:** I, you, he, she (subject pronouns) and their (possessive adjectives) my, your, his, hers.

Demonstrative pronouns are also key grammar components to the beginner lesson and gives your students the ability to indicate or show something in the English language. You can also combine a lesson discussing demonstrative pronouns with singular and plural practice.

✓ **Example:** This, that (singular form) and these, those (plural form).

Important vocabulary objectives useful for beginner student discovery:

The alphabet and number structure is an excellent place to begin when discussing vocabulary in a beginner lesson for obvious reasons. A lesson in the alphabet and learning the basic numbers are keys to the foundation of writing, reading and of course speaking. You can utilize these lessons and combine them with pronunciation, reading, writing, and the grammar objectives discussed above for the beginner student.

✓ **Example:** Ask your students to spell their emails to you as you write it on the board or in a messaging system (for online lessons) in English, you will be surprised by the number of students that have difficulties with this.

Discussing countries, nationalities and native languages can also be a fun and fruitful lesson for the beginner student. Often, countries and other native languages are pronounced and spelled much differently than in English and it is important for your students to get an excellent grasp on this material. This can also be paired nicely with pronunciation and writing as each student takes a country, learns and expresses that countries name, nationality and language spoke to the class. This can also be a great group exercise when teaching more than 4 students.

✓ **Example:** Spain (country), Spanish (nationality), and Spanish (language).

Learning the days of the week is also important for the beginner student and can also help you as a teacher explain tasks and homework deadlines after they are able to put Monday through Sunday into their mental calendar. Your students will have exceptional leaps and bounds in their language discovery once they fully understand the days of the week and it will lay the foundation for learning more about time and months in later lessons.

✓ **Example:** Format the days of the week in a time format that they can understand and this may allow you to briefly describe past, present and future while incorporating yesterday, today and tomorrow into the lesson.

Describing and understanding careers are also key to the beginner skill set and it is also a great opportunity for the students to begin expressing themselves and begin putting together simple sentences.

For young beginners, you can ask students what their parents do for a living and most will be able to describe it in some fun fashion. Don't forget to focus on pronunciation while discussing important words that will help the student build on later when building more complex sentences. Correcting mistakes will be discussed in a later chapter, but remember that it's easier to start good habits than to break bad ones.

  ✓ **Example:** Doctor, lawyer, janitor. I am (subject pronoun with verb *to be*) a doctor.

The family tree and discussing family is important to your students and they will enjoy and discover amazing new ways to talk and tell others about their son or daughter that just completed high school or the new video game a young beginner's father just gave him or her for their birthday. Most students are taking English to express themselves in a new language and most people have and enjoy talking about their families. Build family trees in class and have your students begin using those possessive pronouns to describe their family members.

  ✓ **Example:** Mother, father, brother, son, daughter, great-grandfather, aunt, uncle. My father is a lawyer (possessive pronoun use with job and family vocabulary).

Vocabulary for objects and areas of the house, office, and classroom are also great discovery points for beginners and is a lot of fun to teach and learn. Start your students off with what's in their immediate surroundings, what they can touch, see and feel. This will help them commit these objects to memory with the appropriate English vocabulary. Complementing this lesson with pronunciation and writing is another great way to help your students gain a whole perspective into their new English vocabulary for that lesson. You can also assign your beginner students homework encompassing the objects they have in each room of their home or office.

✓ **Example:** Utilize visual aids for these objects whether they be in the classroom or on a slide presentation. It will help your students see, hear and put it all together easier. I have a television in my bedroom. My house has two bathrooms.

The Elementary Student

The beginner student could be referred to as the noun student and the elementary student could be noted as the verb student in the sense that at the elementary level, your students will become more apt to asking questions to others using verbs. Elementary students can also begin to develop vocabulary surrounding action while combining their simple sentences of nouns and subjects with verbs that will bring their language to life. Towards the end of the elementary level, students are able to ask others questions, answer questions, discuss actions within their daily routines, and develop an overall understanding of past, present, and future times. More complex knowledge comes with more separation between some students and as an EFL teacher, you must be prepared for keeping your lesson plan on track while adapting to the needs of the students that may require a little extra explanation.

Important grammar objectives useful for elementary student discovery:

Understanding the verb *to be* in past and future simple forms are important for your students and will help them develop their ability to put time into a linear format in English. With this language discovery, your students will be able to express their life and experiences in an understandable way to all speakers of English. It is the cornerstone to communication and will set them on the right path when more complex verb tense appears later. Challenge your students to combine previous lesson notes with the new past and future forms of the verb *to be*.

  ✓ **Example:** Was, were, will be, going to be. I am a student (beginner verb *to be* form). I was a student, but now I am an engineer (past simple verb *to be* form).

A student's ability to use can in the positive and negative form is also essential for their self-expression within English. It allows them to tell others what they can or can't do and also gives them the important skill of using their subject pronouns when describing the abilities of others. This lesson can also be used to introduce the positive and negative forms of the past and future simple forms of the verb *to be* described above. I was a student (positive) or I wasn't a student (negative). In your lesson plan outline, which we will go into more detail about later, you can choose what parts you would like to incorporate depending on lesson time and the student's ability to comprehend the material.

✓ **Example:** Can, can't, was, wasn't, were, weren't. I can spell my name, but she can't (positive and negative ability).

The introduction of regular verbs and their past simple forms is essential for the elementary student to grasp while developing new vocabulary and discussing their daily routines and life experiences. This lesson can also be used for the introduction to the positive and negative forms of verbs and how they can be used in a sentence when discussing basic daily concepts. Verbs are important for the elementary student and are the action pieces to their English learning. As a teacher, think about all the different verbs you use in the course of one day and emphasize that to your students, really getting the importance of the verbs and their forms across.

✓ **Example:** Play (regular verb), played (past simple form). I play baseball (regular verb in positive form), I don't play baseball (regular verb in negative form).

Talking about the future is another major part of the English language and your elementary students need to have a good understanding of how to talk and ask questions about the future. Future simple tense is another aspect within the elementary level and it will give your students more confidence to talk about their future goals and aspirations with others and also allow them to have the knowledge to discuss the future within a group setting. A good practice is to challenge your student's ability to formulate more complex sentences about the future after presenting the key points behind the future simple form. The objective is to get your students motivated to use their current knowledge of nouns, verbs and other previous lesson points within their sentences.

✓ **Example:** She will go, he will go, I will go, will you go. She will go to the movies with me on Saturday. Will you go with Tim to the park tomorrow?

Quantities are other important attributes associated with the elementary level and will help your student ask and refer to things in a grammatically correct way. This lesson is often a work in progress for some students since the confusion of much and many can be hard to grasp at first. Make sure you convey this material in a clear way and use visuals to help your students understand the concepts behind quantities in the English language. This is a great lesson for group work and having your students ask and answer questions while using their previously learned discovery points.

✓ **Example:** Some, any, a lot, how much, how many. Get those visuals out and really emphasize each individual point. I have some. I don't have any. How much is that car? How many rooms are in your house?

When discussing frequency adverbs, it is important to develop them around language they can understand at the elementary level while using what they know in combination with the frequency adverb they intend to use. This is another great opportunity to get your student or students engaged in open conversation about their daily routines. A good practice for this lesson is to set the frequency adverbs on a percentage scale from 0% to 100% allowing them to see the frequency in which each frequency adverb is commonly used. You can also give them choices of correct frequency adverb sentences against incorrect frequency adverb sentences in order to monitor their understanding of the material.

✓ **Example:** Never 0%, Rarely 20%, Occasionally 40%, Sometimes 50%, Usually 60%, Frequently 80%, Always

100%. I always brush my teeth in the morning. I occasionally have time to exercise after work.

Important vocabulary objectives useful for elementary student discovery:

Beginning elementary level vocabulary with months, years and dates will complement the days of the week and the numbers 0-100 perfectly. Your elementary student will be able to put his/her past language discovery together with something new and this will help build confidence and can also be a great group exercise. **This lesson can also be paired with telling time and setting appointments** if the classroom time and schedule allows for it.

   ✓ **Example:** January 1st, 2009 is New Year's Day. Have your students right this, pronounce it and even engage other students in conversation in a question and answer format.

Discussing vocabulary for weather is also an important attribute for the elementary level and this will help the student describe days and even have the confidence to engage in some basic conversation about days, weather and so on. Pairing this lesson with simple sentences can also allow for group and individual participation.

✓ **Example:** It was raining yesterday, but today it is sunny. Last winter was cold.

Another excellent lesson for your elementary students is basic descriptions of buildings and places (like the pharmacy or bank). This is a useful exercise that can be used with many previous language discoveries like daily routines, careers and will also compliment another elementary level task which is **giving and following directions** when going from one place to another. Focus on street names, direction (north, south, etc…) and also left and right can be introduced by showing the students the "L" your fingers make when holding out just your thumb and index finger.

✓ **Example:** My mom works at the hospital on Main Street, just past the bank on the right (in description form). To go to the pharmacy, take a right on Main Street and a left on 12th Avenue. The pharmacy will be on your left (giving directions).

Using basic adjectives are also part of the elementary student's skill set. Knowing the colors, old, new, good, bad are all important opposite adjectives that can help your students take another step in language discovery and conversation as they begin to gain confidence in describing the things around them. Use a lot of visual examples in this lesson to really get the points across and encourage them to participate as much as possible.

✓ **Example:** Point out things in the classroom or in a slideshow and ask your students to use those new adjectives to describe what they see. Remember, it is important to get this right the first time, because it will be frustrating for your students later if they fall behind in later lessons.

The elementary student will also begin to learn about comparative adjectives and it will be a great time to compare things that the student now can describe using the previously discovered basic adjectives. Your students should be able to easily compare two things by the end of this lesson and this could be a great lesson plan goal for a possible lesson in your future!

✓ **Example:** My pencil is bigger than my teacher's pencil. Today is nicer than yesterday. Use the previously discovered language to help your students put the whole package together. This will boost their confidence and also help them review some key points from previous lessons.

The Pre-Intermediate Student

This is often the level at which you will see your students begin to blossom if you have been instructing them for a while. The pre-intermediate level is a special time for the student, when they can take all the language discoveries of the previous lessons and begin to share their thoughts. All the confidence building combined with their ability to formulate sentences with a clear understanding of grammar will enable them to discuss topics relating to the future and their experiences.

Your students will gain access to another set of vocabulary that will help them express travel, free time activities and things they like or don't like to do. It's a special time and if you as a teacher layer the foundation for them properly, you will have the satisfaction of more insightful conversations with someone whom once sat across a table a just looked at you without the ability to speak. Unfortunately, teaching English can have its pitfalls and you may step into a situation where some students did not receive the proper foundation. Utilize your knowledge in what each previous level should already know and take your time getting everyone up to speed. Patience is an EFL virtue.

Important grammar objectives useful for pre-intermediate student discovery:

The pre-intermediate student will begin their journey into possessive pronouns and can be used to compliment what they discovered in their beginner lessons regarding subject pronouns. Possessive pronouns will give them the confidence to begin expressing what is theirs or what belongs to someone else. Utilize this in conjunction with the vocabulary they discovered in previous lessons. Incorporation and language checking is an important way for you as a teacher to assess what your students are retaining.

- ✓ **Example:** Today is my birthday. October 12th is my father's birthday.

Discussing adverbs is also part of the pre-intermediate skill set and it will help them describe things with even more emphasis. Adverbs are "commonly" confused with adjectives, so it is important for you as the teacher to explain the differences and ways to use the adverbs. Build on what they know, starting with the frequency adverbs they had previously discovered and work your way through it using examples and remember to double check their understanding of this lesson. When some students get discouraged they become silent and try to hide, challenge them to break out of their shells and gain confidence to overcome.

- ✓ **Example:** I **always** brush my teeth in the morning (frequency adverb). I **accidentally** spilled my coffee. I **silently** walked home from school.

Another important part of the pre-intermediate student's language discovery is the use of irregular verbs in past simple tense. Irregular verbs when discussed in past simple tense can be very difficult at first, but in time with some great guidance and a lot of examples, your students will gain confidence and begin using them without thinking. Begin with a list of verbs, both irregular and regular and work your way down letting your student or students discover the correct forms before intervening. Natural discovery can allow them to build confidence and can give your student a little more control. Most students know the past simple tense of irregular verbs without even knowing they are irregular.

> ✓ **Example:** Walk (walked), work (worked), run (ran), swim (swam). I ran to the park to see my friends (incorporation of previously discovered language in a sentence form).

The pre-intermediate student will also begin discussing past continuous and present perfect tense. You can often put the tenses together in one lesson if you have enough time to thoroughly cover each tense adequately. As a teacher it is up to you to decide what and how much your students or student can handle.

> ✓ **Example:** I was walking home when I heard the news (past continuous).

Important vocabulary objectives useful for pre-intermediate student discovery:

Talking about surroundings and landscape is very important and will help your student to piece together some of the things they may want to describe in relation to past experiences and future plans. This is a fun lesson that can be incorporated with beautiful pictures and give students a chance to present some of their new words in a way to describe what they have done and what they plan to do in front of the class or to the teacher.

> ✓ **Example:** River, lake, ocean, sea, mountain. I **lived** (past simple verb) in the **mountains** (landscape vocabulary) when I was **younger** (comparative). Let your students use their arsenal of vocabulary and grammar knowledge, set them free a little here.

Discussing and describing clothing is a huge part of everyday life and it is important the your pre-intermediate students understand what is what. Use visuals and keep the discussion flowing as they discover new vocabulary relating to everyday life. You can use this lesson to revisit adjectives, comparatives, adverbs and anything else you can think of to do a secret check on what they are retaining from previous lessons.

✓ **Example:** Pants, socks, shirt, T-shirt, suit, tie. Tommy has a blue shirt and brown pants (use of adjectives with new vocabulary).

Letting your students discover language that will assist them in discussing their hobbies and what they are interested in is also a key aspect of the pre-intermediate level. This is what makes this level so much fun, allowing your students to really explain and express their interests is important in conversation and will build their confidence. Put this lesson together with timelines to reintroduce time, past, present and future. Group participation, writing and the use of visuals are all great components to partner with this lesson. This could be a great opportunity to also assign presentation homework for the student to work on and share with the class the next day or on a Monday.

✓ **Example:** I like to **draw**. I usually **draw** after school after doing my homework. I enjoy **hiking** on the weekends with my friends.

More great vocabulary to consider when planning a pre-intermediate lesson is body parts. This can be often overlooked since we don't normally talk about body parts on a routine basis, however, it remains a key aspect. Your student's ability to discuss body parts can assist them in explaining what is wrong to a doctor in a foreign country and may also give them the vocabulary they need to describe an experience or feeling. This lesson is great with the use of visual aids and/or a slideshow and can be a fun day of pointing to areas of the body and trying to pronounce the designated words. You can also introduce to your student some common health issues that they can associate with specific body parts while also using non-verbal communication.

✓ **Example:** Eyes, ears, stomach, throat, head. I have a **headache**. My **stomach** is upset.

Knowing the superlative adds to the comparative lesson your students previously had and it will give them the ability to not only compare two things, but compare multiple objects, places, feelings, etc… You can also have your students practice with some of their previously discovered words and reintroduce the "syllable rule" when discussing superlatives and comparatives to really drive home the lesson.

✓ **Example:** Nice (Nicest), beautiful (most beautiful). My house is the nicest in the neighborhood.

The Intermediate Student

The intermediate level can often be viewed as the most difficult to keep your students engaged and enthusiastic when it comes to their language discovery. They have been learning English for some time now and can communicate on a basic level with other native and non-native English speakers. They have the basic language skill set that will allow them to strike up conversation, make reservations and even travel internationally with more confidence since English has become a global language. When beginning your intermediate lessons, it is imperative for you to think about relevancy and really start addressing each student's goals and needs. Making their learning relevant will allow them to continue making progress toward their goals and help them compliment their basic communication skills with power and flow in their fluency.

Important grammar objectives useful for intermediate student discovery:

Adding tense discovery with past present continuous is a great way to keep your intermediate student's minds working efficiently and will add some needed language discovery at this level. Present perfect continuous will allow your student to discuss things in a duration minded way, duration from the past until this moment. It will also give them the skill set to discuss what they have been doing recently in a more knowledgeable way.

- ✓ **Example:** I have been working at the hospital for five years (duration until this moment). Have you been to the map lately (events in a recent timeline)?

The past perfect tense is also another valuable tool for an intermediate student and it can also be used for language discovery purposes to keep your students engaged at this level. Past perfect can often be a surprising new twist to the English language at first, but with a good lesson plan and great examples mixed with some student participation, it can be a fun and informative class. There are a few different ways to use past perfect and they can all be a little confusing at first, so you can benefit from starting your students off with some key examples. An action that occurred before something in the past and duration of time before something in the past in a non-continuous form are good places to start.

- ✓ **Example:** I had never seen a sunset before last night. By the time she finished writing, she had been sitting for six hours.

The use of more modal verbs is also a great way to keep your students language discovery moving in a positive direction. Modal verbs are important and unique for your intermediate student to understand a bit more about. Your students may already know a few modal verbs from the earlier levels when piecing together structured sentences and adding a few more with some rules attached will keep them enthused and allow them to understand modal verb usage more by the time they have finished you lesson full of excellent examples and class participation.

- ✓ **Example:** Should, shall, can, could, may, might, must. He **may** or **may not** (the use of not in present and past forms with modal verbs) come with us to the movies.

The introduction of conditionals is also a great way to get your intermediate students on the path to more language discovery. Conditionals are fun and will allow your students to discuss things in a "what if" type of conversation. These conversations and discussions are very common in the English language and are important for your students to understand and have the ability to construct. We all know the conditional, "If I win the lottery, I would…" Introducing great examples with conditional clauses paired with the main clauses is important and then you can progress into the first, second and third conditional forms. Lots of examples equal better results in this lesson.

- ✓ **Example:** If I win the lottery (conditional clause), I will buy a new house and sports car (main clause). You can complement this with all the vocabulary your students have previously discovered making for a fun class of creativity and imagination.

Important vocabulary objectives useful for intermediate student discovery:

Focusing on vocabulary discovered through reading and listening comprehension exercises will keep your students engaged and tested. Your intermediate students will begin understanding movies, articles and books since they have developed so many new grammar and vocabulary skills and can begin thinking more critically about topics. You can let your student read articles out loud and let them discover new words and phrases naturally. The key here is to make sure you check in with them every few paragraphs and ask them if they have any questions. A good indicator of a new vocabulary word is when your student stops on a word when reading and new words are often mispronounced. Remember to keep your material relevant to your student's goals and interests so they stay engaged.

> ✓ **Example:** find an article of interest to your student and review it together. Let them read and develop new questions and discover new vocabulary. Natural Discovery! Remember to let then read and talk as much as they can and ask insightful questions about the material.

Your student's ability to understand the ages and stages of life is also very important at the intermediate level. This will allow them to discuss and identify the different areas of life and will help them to grow confidence in an otherwise skipped area of learning. When many learners of English or any language begin their studies, the last thing on their mind is the different stages in life. This exercise will allow your students to realize that there is still English to learn and become more energized and enthusiastic. Remember, the intermediate level is where your students will see less natural discovery, but as a teacher, it is imperative to keep them engaged in every exercise and lesson.

✓ **Example:** Utilize examples of age and the different vocabulary associated with that age (teenager is 13 to 18 years old). You can use many pictures of famous people from their home country to get them even more engaged in the material. This can also be paired with writing exercises and sentence construction.

Transitional words and phrases come in all shapes and sizes and are extremely important for the intermediate student to have a good understanding of. These transition words are used in everyday speech, reading and writing. There are so many different types of transition words and phrases and each have their own category. Transitional words can address time, place, comparisons, contrasts, effects, causes and the list goes on. Your students most likely know some transitional words and phrases already, but as we know as

English teachers, there are so many more out there to learn and teach. This lesson can be a one day or two day lesson depending on the time of each class. It can be paired with speech, group activity, writing and open participation.

- ✓ **Example:** Transitional words for the category **Addition** (furthermore, moreover, also, in addition, besides). In addition to his research, Dr. Hartman is also involved in his community.

The Upper-Intermediate Student

There is a thin line between the intermediate and upper-intermediate level and it is always a great idea to do some in class checks to see where your student or students are in according with the language level guidelines. One thing that is frustrating to some students is when they think they are at one level, but really are a bit lower. Before awarding any level credential, it is essential to double check the knowledge and fluency of your student before benchmarking any past progress. That being said, your upper-intermediate student has a vast knowledge of vocabulary and can read, write and most importantly communicate with a somewhat natural level of fluency. Your upper-intermediate students will have the ability to hold formal and informal conversations and have the skill set to differentiate the appropriate vocabulary in each varied setting.

Important grammar objectives useful for upper-intermediate student discovery:

Past perfect continuous is a great place to start at the upper-intermediate level and may allow your students to not only discover something new in English, but also feel engaged and still rewarded for their time spent in class. Some students will grasp the concept of past perfect continuous easier than others, so be prepared to challenge those students while still staying within your lesson plan. Past perfect continuous shows **duration before something in the past happened** and also a **cause of something in the past**. Some students may know only one of the two ways this tense is used, so it's important to clearly define and give examples of both.

✓ **Example:** Tom had been working for two years before he left for Europe (duration before something in the past happened). Cathy was tired because she had been working all day (cause of something in the past).

Another excellent tense for the upper intermediate level is future perfect. Again, it is important to make sure that both uses for future perfect are explained well before allowing your students to construct ideas and stenches around the material. If they learn it the right way the first time, they will not develop bad habits or begin confusing it with another tense in an unrelated situation. Future perfect has two forms and two uses. The two forms are **Will** and **Be Going To** and they express a **completed action before something in the future** and also the **duration before a future event**. You can combine this lesson with writing assignments and group work and can also dive into passive and active forms of this tense as well.

✓ **Example:** By next year, I will have completed my TEFL course (completed action before a future event). I will have been here for 8 hours by the time I leave (duration before a future event). They will have completed the test before the time is up (active form). The test will have been completed before time is up (passive).

Having the knowledge to use reported speech in English is a very valuable tool for your upper intermediate to fully grasp. Reported speech allows your student to report what someone else has said in many different categories like statements, questions and requests. Your students will be able to take direct speech and transform it into indirect speech in order to complete this learning objective. Some of your students may have some knowledge of how to do this already since it is natural for humans to learn how to discuss others naturally, but brainstorm and find ways to challenge those students within your lesson plan. This is a great class participation and group exercise and can also be used with individual students if paired with audio, giving them a chance to indirectly report on what was said by someone else. This is also a great opportunity for listening comprehension.

✓ **Example:** "I run every morning before work (direct speech)." She said that she goes running every morning before work (indirect transformation). This example is a statement, so remember that reported speech can be used in questions and requests as well.

Passive verb form lessons are also great for keeping your upper intermediate students engaged and continuing to discover new vocabulary and grammar. Teaching passive verb forms can be a fun lesson and will engage your students on many different levels depending on your well thought out lesson plan. Starting with the basics of passive verb forms, begin by differentiating the difference between active and passive. This lesson can then move into using the active and passive verb form sentences in the various tenses that have been previously taught or by even adding a few more new ones at this time. An **active** form consists of, **(thing doing an action + verb + thing receiving the action)**. The **passive** form consists of, **(thing receiving the action + be + past form of verb + by + thing doing the action)**.

✓ **Example:** Once a week, Tara cleans the kitchen (active, present simple tense). Once a week, the kitchen is cleaned by Tara (passive, present simple tense).

Important vocabulary objectives useful for upper-intermediate student discovery:

In today's technological society, the world has become relatively small and as some of you will soon find out, English can be taught to students all over the world via the internet. Your students will have vast knowledge of **science and technology** in their native language and it is imperative that they are also able to express and discuss those same scientific and technological subjects in English. These vocabulary areas have become so common place in our languages that the importance of communicating with this vocabulary is imperative for the upper intermediate student. This lesson can have great importance for your adult students since many of them ma work in tech fields. Younger students also have knowledge of technology and science, most of them can show you any application on their smartphones or tablets that they may bring to class to distract themselves from their learning. Utilize examples and make it relevant to what is going on today, not 10 years ago, because science and technology is an ever changing topic.

  √ **Example:** Use online magazines that discuss new experiments and technology that will engage your students in conversation and allow for natural discovery of new words and phrases.

Going back over feelings is also an important part of the upper intermediate vocabulary and though they should have happy and sad figured out, challenge them to expand their vocabulary so they can begin pushing out those academic, graduate school words we all disliked thinking about during SAT and GRE testing. Go with what they know and show them how they can expand these words to help them sound more educated and knowledgeable. This will give them confidence to spark new conversations with new people in their daily lives. Introduce these new words, construct sentences and allow your students to get creative.

 ✓ **Example:** Happy (basic feeling vocabulary), cheerful or delighted (more powerful vocabulary surrounding feelings). I was delighted to see so many people at the grand opening of my store.

Discussing personality and the use of more expanded adjectives in speech and writing will also allow your students to feel more confident in conversation and also help them to develop greater reading and writing skills. Some of your students may be ready to begin reading more academic type journals or even more fluent newspapers with extravagant words written by well educated, knowledgeable authors. The upper intermediate student needs to be able to express personality in a new way and this lesson is a great way to keep them engaged in new material and also build more communication confidence. You can pair this lesson with so many other skills, just be sure to watch time and relevancy when building your lesson plan.

- ✓ **Example:** The man was very **thrifty** and was able to save for a new car without taking a loan. The dinner party was **elegant**. Challenge your students to describe things around them in a different way than before.

Being able to discuss medical issues is another great skill for your upper intermediate students to possess. You may have briefly touched on some common medical issues when teaching body parts to your lower level students, but now it is time to get a little more in-depth. Keep in mind, unless they are medical students, it is best to not go overboard with medical terminology. The best way to keep this lesson relevant and fun is to think about the past five years of your life and write down all the medical issues you, a friend or family member may have had. If it is common in your life, than most likely, it will be common and relevant for your students. Have your students develop a story after you show them some examples and give them some base vocabulary to work with.

- ✓ **Example:** Last year I had a **sore throat** and the doctor gave me **antibiotics** and **pain medication** to help me through it. I had to take two days **sick leave** from work and the **pain**

medication made me **nauseated** and **light headed**. I also developed a **rash** (eight new words in one short paragraph).

The Advanced Student

The advanced student has a wide range of grammar and vocabulary knowledge and has the confidence to start up a conversation with almost any native speaker from any country. The advanced student has earned his level over years of trial and error within communication and has often put several years into his or her English language goals. The advanced student is generally able to discuss almost any topic in English with fluent structure of a native English speaker, but may be lost when it comes to idioms, specific phrases, metaphors and similes. This is where you can sharpen your advanced teaching skills and really get at the heart of your student's goals and aspirations as it relates to English language discovery.

An important thing to remember at this level is teacher talk time. Your student can often have a lot in common with you, but it is important to maintain the lesson plan and don't let the lesson turn into a Sunday afternoon conversation over coffee, unless that is what your student wants. Always remember to make an excellent lesson plan that will engage and inspire your student to continue his path on

English discovery. Keep building that confidence and don't forget to keep things relevant to your student at this level.

Important grammar objectives useful for advanced student discovery:

When thinking about your advanced student's language discovery, a good place to begin is future perfect continuous. Introducing more complex tenses at this level will allow your advanced student to realize that there are some new grammar points out there in English left to be discovered. The future perfect continuous form has two forms, **Will** and **Be Going To**, similar to future perfect, only with different uses. You can use future perfect continuous to describe **duration before a future event** and also the **cause of a future event**. Examples are crucial in this lesson and expand on the different forms using class or group participation and developing some new writing skills that support the lesson material. This can also be paired with passive and active voice as well as proper adverb placement.

- ✓ **Example:** They **will have been waiting** for two hours by the time she arrives (duration before a future event). Billy will be tired when he gets home because he will have been working for over 12 hours (cause of a future event).

Another excellent skill for your advanced students to have in their English tool kit are the use of question tags. Question tags are often used in communication, but rarely utilized in written form, so this lesson is all about participation and practice. A question tag is a question form that comes after a statement in order to keep a conversation moving. I believe that most native speakers do this with little thought and it is a grammar point an advanced student can utilize when conversing with native speakers. The flow of a conversation is important and when it becomes stagnant, a non-native English speaker may lose confidence and possibly end the conversational all together. As a teacher, we must not only teach the grammar and vocabulary points. We must also build confidence and give our students the relative communication skills to be successful in any area. This can be paired with relevant topics your students are interested in and it is a good way for them to really hone their conversation skills. Rule of thumb for question tags, negative statements require positive tags and positive statements require negative tags.

    ✓ **Example:** That car is a classic, isn't it (positive to negative tag)? They didn't leave yet, did they (negative to positive tag)?

Getting back in touch with prefixes and suffixes is another excellent way to keep the flow of language discovery moving in the right direction. The grammar world of prefixes and suffixes can often be left out while other things pop up along the way, but returning to it can surprise your student and their knowledge of them may also surprise you as well. With a little research, you can create a lesson plan that will be informative and structured. Explain the most common prefixes and suffixes and then work your way to others, engaging your students with examples and communication on what they think is the proper suffix or prefix for a designated word. Some may surprise them and this lesson is also a perfect time to check-in on pronunciation.

- ✓ **Example:** Semi (prefix), half (prefix meaning), semicircle (word with prefix). Check pronunciation and have them use it in a sentence. This is also a great word to get the class up and moving by asking them to form a semicircle.

Important vocabulary objectives useful for advanced student discovery:

Metaphors are extremely important for the advanced student since their daily conversation may be with native English speakers in a new country or at work. The use of metaphors are prevalent in writing, reading, and definitely in speech. Your student can dive into the world of native English metaphors by reading or listening to interviews and they may know a few, but it is also important that you make sure that a metaphor they want to use is appropriate and relevant to the time. Take some time and research some common metaphors and develop a list you would like to address in your lesson. It might be rewarding to ask your students if they know any at first before showing what you have in store for them. Some students may have knowledge of a few metaphors, but the definition of the word metaphor may not be known. These are all things to keep in mind when developing your lesson plan.

> ✓ **Example:** Roller coaster of emotions (common metaphor). What does it mean? How and when can you use it?

The advanced level is also a level for discovering and understanding idioms. Idioms are often strange and foreign to non-native English speakers, because of the way native speakers learn idioms in the first place. There is no general ideology behind idioms; they just naturally happen in our environment over time, often expressed by family, friends, radio, movies and television. Again, it is extremely important to make sure that the idioms are relevant to the time and also appropriate. There have been many idioms used and deemed inappropriate as well as corny or old. An idiom lesson should be fun and there should be animation to your instruction. This is a great time for non-verbal communication and the use of body language to get the idiom across. Have a fun and informative lesson with idioms and help your students build more confidence and discover new things at such a high level.

- ✓ **Example:** Piece of cake (idiom). What do you think it means? This can be a fun engagement between you and your students.

Student Level Concluded

The student levels above outline what your students should be capable of as they progress in their goals and English language discovery. Again, this is just a brief outline to help you begin understanding the different levels within EFL and how you can approach each level with a knowledgeable understanding of the student's basic needs. An emphasis on your student's goals and keeping things relevant are key factors in developing a great lesson plan that is fitted to your class and student's level. Remember to be adaptable and know that sometimes you need to change gears and adjust the lesson accordingly. As you continue reading and discovering the aspects of EFL, you will enhance your knowledge with more in-depth material involving lesson development that will not only give you the skills to teach, but also the confidence and mental strategy to plan an excellent lesson.

Chapter Two

Keeping Lessons Relevant and Controlled

Chapter Overview:

Relevant Teaching is Relevant Learning

Scaling Lesson Material

Outlining Aims and Objectives

Talking Time and Length

Relevant Teaching is Relevant Learning

In the previous section we discussed a lot of different key aspects you can utilize for teaching your students on various English levels. You may have noticed some particular important phrasing I used, "keep your lesson relevant." This may be one of the most important parts of teaching English to non-native speakers of all ages, professions, academic standings, and English levels. Relevancy is the cornerstone to having a successful lesson and without it your students will get lost, bored, and become increasingly frustrated and unenthused by your material, no matter how important or well planned. If there were a "step one, two, and three method" to learning English as a foreign language, it would be to know your student's English level, interests and goals, develop an excellent lesson plan, and make all material and exercises relevant.

If you have a student who is a beginner and his or her career is accounting, the challenge of relevancy can become difficult to figure out. Getting to know your students in your first class together is not time lost. Don't think that you have to go right into bookwork, colors, and so on. Take time to get to know your student's life, goals, hobbies, travel destinations, family, friends, what they do on weekends or after work during the week. Taking the first lesson to build a foundation is extremely important and will allow you to develop superb lessons in the following months, keeping your students engaged in the material and lesson you worked so diligently to prepare. This first meeting is also a great opportunity to build rapport and a key time to check what his or her English ability truly is.

Asking simple conversation questions is not just for the sake of conversation, but in some ways a journalistic interview. This precious time is important and feel free to share with your student why you want to know more about him or her. Informing your student about building solid foundations and the importance of relevancy will possibly help your student open up even more. They want to learn English and feel good about spending money to do it, so communicate with your students and let them in on your plans, most of them will appreciate the fact you have a plan, something some teachers do not have or utilize. The beginner English student who is a professional accountant and enjoys traveling to scuba diving destinations and running marathons can have so much relevant material to choose from.

As an example, choose a popular diving destination and research what is there and begin your creative teacher thinking to build a beginner lesson plan. Introduce the question words and the expletives and then introduce main areas of the diving destination. With all the information explained to your student, begin asking some basic questions using the newly discovered question words and have your student answer using the newly discovered expletives. Relevancy, relevancy, and more relevancy.

Creative Teacher Thinking

How could you plan a lesson for an intermediate student who is an architect and enjoys playing golf with friends and colleagues on the weekends and also enjoys traveling for marathon races?

Scaling Lesson Material

Scaling or grading your lesson material is a step by step incline from easy to difficult as the lesson and material progresses. A good way to think about scaling is to imagine yourself climbing a hill and how a gradual, easy start can be beneficial for the overall goal of accomplishment, making it to the top of the hill without serious injury or bodily stress. It is often similar for your students and you do not want them to be exhausted before the end message of the material is delivered. Scaling is also a very important part of building confidence in your students as they move forward and begin completing a few of their short term English goals. If the hill begins with a cliff face that the student needs ropes and harnesses to climb, than your student will become frustrated and possibly give up and develop a bad taste for learning English.

Nobody wants to feel inadequate, frustrated or stressed out when doing anything. Kids can overcome this easier, but if your student is an accomplished surgeon who has several academic papers published in his or her native language, feeling inadequate will destroy your rapport and the student may find a new teacher or give up on English all together. Build your student's confidence and begin with easy material that will develop into more challenging exercises as the lesson or week progresses. One good method to scaling is to start with the outer shell and slowly crack it open to reveal more complex parts within the basic outer layer.

For example, a car is a good outer shell and is relevant to most students from most regions of the world. After car, open the door and let the inner vocabulary begin pouring out, but again, engine parts are not as relevant as horn or turn signal. Utilize things that they are familiar with or already know first and always be sure to explain how to fully complete a task using key examples or a guideline, really getting the message and task across before assigning your students a similar task of their own. Remember your scale and keep your student's confidence building to maximum levels.

Another aspect of scaling when planning your lesson and giving your students tasks to complete at home or during class time are the components of the task assigned. Let's go back to our beginner level student who is an accountant that enjoys traveling to scuba diving destinations. Simply asking him to write two short paragraphs on his favorite diving destination could be a task with insufficient information to complete. As a teacher, it is essential for you to understand what is needed to complete the task you have asked your student to complete. So what would be the working parts of this specific task? First define what tense he should be writing in (present simple), sentence structure will be important, adjectives, expletives, and of course the outline for two paragraphs describing something of interest. All of these components must be taught before the task can be given in order to ensure excellent scaling and confidence to complete the task.

Creative Teacher Thinking

What would be another example of scaling in order for your elementary students to successfully complete a writing task that involves writing an email explaining a recent vacation?

Here is a great example to follow:

- ✓ A good format to follow is to first think about the English grammar and vocabulary that will surround the task.
- ✓ After you ensure that is well understood by your students, give them an example email so they can see the format and style of how the email should be put together.
- ✓ Have your students begin thinking about places they have vacationed and what they saw or experienced (you can write some of their thoughts on the board).
- ✓ You can break up the board into parts (places, sights, experiences, adjectives, and verbs).
- ✓ Again, at the end of the instruction and board work, reintroduce an email relating to the task and take questions to ensure all students are ready to begin writing.

Outlining Aims and Objectives

This is an important area of lesson planning and will help you and your students stay on task during lesson time. Having clear aims and objectives will allow you and your student to understand what outcome is wanted for the lesson material and what areas that will be covered in order to achieve the desired outcome.

Let's put this into perspective by examining an elementary student lesson:

The time has come for our elementary level student to begin discovering direction. In this lesson they will learn how to follow, give, and receive directions.

Aim:

- ✓ The aim is for the student to be able to follow simple directions while using a map.

Objectives:

- ✓ Introduction of direction vocabulary (left, right, straight).
- ✓ Introduction of a map and its components (north, south, east, west).
- ✓ Correct sentence structure for directions.
- ✓ Following step by step instructions.

It is also important to share the aims and objectives of your lessons with your students. This will allow them to become more involved and aware of what they should be focusing on and it is also a great tool for us as teachers, allowing us to make sure we are going in the right direction during our lesson. Sharing lesson aims and objectives are also a great way to keep a good line of communication flowing with your students. As a teacher of a foreign language, it is crucial to stay in touch with your students and make sure the communication flow is moving in both directions, building trust, rapport and a healthy student/teacher relationship.

Creative Teacher Thinking

In our previous Creative Teacher Thinking exercise, we discussed how to use scaling when planning a lesson around writing an email. What would be the aims and objectives for a student writing an email about a previous vacation?

Talking Time and Length

This question comes up often in lesson planning and will play an important part of your very own lesson planning when the time arrives. Soon we will go into detail about the Presentation, Practice, and Production (PPP) format that almost all teachers utilize when developing quality lesson plans. One essential part to the PPP format is timing and talk-time. Before we dive into PPP in depth, let's discuss timing your lesson and who should be actually talking during the various stages within your lesson.

Think of PPP as a pyramid and the first stage, the top of the pyramid will be Presentation, the time in the lesson where you the teacher presents the material for the lesson. The top of the pyramid is small and the timing of this part should reflect that. The middle off the pyramid, the Practice part, is slightly larger than the top, so this area of the lesson will be longer in duration. Finally, the base of the pyramid, the production part, is the largest and will also take up most of the lesson's time.

The time spent on each part is of course dictated by how much time you have for the lesson, for example, a one hour lesson will be:

- ✓ Presentation (15 minutes)
- ✓ Practice (20 minutes)
- ✓ Production (25 minutes)

This basic format will allow you to keep time in mind and give you a solid format to follow in order to stay on track and give an exceptional lesson.

Talk time is also a very important aspect in regards to the PPP breakdown of your lesson and has some universal abbreviations all of us teachers use to divide up talk time.

- ✓ T-ST is when the teacher talks or presents material to the students (Presentation).
- ✓ ST-T is when students talk or develop the material with the teacher (Presentation, Practice).
- ✓ ST-ST is when students discuss lesson material amongst themselves (Practice, Production).
- ✓ PR is used for when students are working in pairs (Practice, Production).
- ✓ GR is used for group work and is used for larger classes (Practice, Production).

These abbreviations can allow you to break down each section of your lesson within each part of the PPP format. During Presentation, you will be doing much of the talking so you may think that putting T-ST for the entire Presentation Part is sufficient, but this can lead to bad and lazy teaching habits. Break down your Presentation into sections and dedicate a specific time for each section. For example, introducing vocabulary can be noted as (T-ST 5 minutes) and so on.

Get creative and ensure your lesson plan has a structure that will give you confidence while teaching the lesson.

Chapter Three

Lesson Plan Basics

Chapter Overview:

Developing a PPP Lesson Plan

Presentation Stage

Practice Stage

Production Stage

Teacher Talk Time (TTT)

Lesson Plan Format

Lesson Plan Checklist

Developing a PPP Lesson Plan

The time has come for you to dive into the general components of designing your future, amazing, and informative lesson plans. As you continue further into your TEFL textbook, you will discover that there is much more involved when actually standing in front of a class and delivering the material planned out. This is the beginning phase, an outline and foundation that will give you the tools to begin creatively thinking about some possible lesson plans for your future classes. In the previous section covering timing and talk time, we went over the general definitions regarding Presentation, Practice, and Production, so let's look a little closer into each part of the PPP format.

Presentation Stage

An important thing to remember when developing your PPP lesson plan is the effectiveness in which you teach your material (objectives) in order to get your desired outcome (aim). The Presentation part of your PPP is just that, a presentation where you introduce new material to your students. A great way to go about the introduction of new material is to remember scaling and begin with what they know or are familiar with. Starting with the shell will allow your students to connect with what they know, building confidence and allowing for greater enthusiasm when new vocabulary or grammar begins to pop up.

Another important aspect behind introducing new material to your students is to make sure you do it in an exciting and contextual way. Presenting new material via a few word statements and some black writing on the white board is not a good way to begin a new lesson. You want your students to be excited or intrigued by the new material they are about to discover. This is a very important part of your lesson plan, because it sets the tone for the rest of the lesson time. Use a contextual theme that will spark interest and get your students engaged in the topic. Photos, stories and videos are all excellent ways to introduce new material. Remember to keep it relevant and based off of something they may already be familiar with.

Once the material has now been successfully and clearly delivered it is crucial to take the next step in the Presentation and deconstruct your new material by breaking apart the shell and letting your students see what is inside. Explain the rules, why, how, when, and all the other relevant information surrounding the material you so carefully introduced in an exciting, contextualized way. By breaking it down, you are essentially making your students certified mechanics of that material. They will be able to strip it apart like an engine and put it back together again without a problem. This is your goal for Presentation and after they have become mechanics of the lesson material, open up the floor for discussion and questions in order to make sure that the material has been understood 100% before moving forward. When you begin teaching you will understand the importance of asking your students important questions about the new material as well. Double check and ensure your students understand, especially the quiet ones.

Creative Teacher Thinking

Taking into account the guidelines of Presentation and the importance of using contextualized material, what would be a great way to introduce shopping at the mall vocabulary? Don't forget to spark interest in your students and do some creative thinking surrounding your own shopping experiences.

Practice Stage

The practice stage is an excellent time to take a step back and let the new material sink in through carefully planned and designed tasks and examples. Choose tasks and exercises that will allow your students to really focus on the new material. The exercises should produce ST-ST talk time allowing the teacher to observe and be ready for questions, corrections and naturally discovered teaching points that may develop. You should also encapsulate the material with the exercise, making the main focus of the exercise and discussions to be mainly based on the newly discovered material. The Practice stage is also an excellent time for PR and GR talk time, encouraging your students to communicate and build conversations in English about their new material.

This communication is crucial and is exactly why most students begin taking English language lessons in the first place, in order to communicate in English. Encouraging communication is almost as important as the structure of the task or exercise itself. Make sure you develop an exercise that the student will only be able to successfully complete if he or she really understands the new material. Try to stray away from tasks or exercises that follow patterns that are easy for students to figure out. Another great thing to keep in mind is to keep the exercise relevant to life and normal conversation. Most textbooks and English language learning websites will use generic non-contextual tasks that can easily be completed. Remember the guidelines of the lesson scale and structure each exercise to be more challenging than the one before it.

For example, utilizing a question and answer structure that relates to the new material while also referring back to a story or maybe some pictures you used to introduce the new material in the Presentation stage. Our shopping at the mall scenario may have had some pictures designated to introduce new vocabulary.

- ✓ **Question** (teacher structure): How much was the pink sweater in the first picture?
- ✓ **Answer** (student fills it in): The pink sweater costs $23.00.

You can even reverse the roles and have the student fill in a question that would match a given answer. This makes them think about the new material in different ways and helps them visualize the material in a way that will relate to their everyday lives. Remember to encourage communication and let them compare and ask ash other questions about the new material and the tasks.

Creative Teacher Thinking

Why is Practice so important and in a two hour lesson, how much time should be allocated to the Practice stage in respect to the Presentation, Practice, and Production (PPP) pyramid structure.

Production Stage

By the time you have worked through your exceptionally developed lesson plan and slid down the PPP pyramid to the production stage, your students have had an informative and contextual introduction and had time to practice their new material with others. Your students should be veteran mechanics when it comes to their newly discovered material and have practiced taking it apart and putting it back together several times now while communicating with others and completing the material focused exercises.

The Production stage is an important time for your students to take the new material and run with it on their own. As the teacher you decide how they will deliver their new knowledge, but they will put it together themselves since they have had plenty of previous practice. Having your students do a presentation on the new material or developing a short writing on the material would be beneficial Production exercises. We will discuss the Production stage in more detail later, but begin to think about what might be a good Production stage exercise.

Creative Teacher Thinking

Without any real concrete knowledge of the Production stage and what might be a good way for your students to produce, describe what you think would be beneficial for student Production regarding new material in a scenario and English level of your choice.

Teacher Talk Time (TTT)

Teacher Talk Time (TTT) is something English language teachers are constantly discussing when it comes to presenting and giving your student the important information he or she needs for that particular lesson. There is a basic principle to keep in mind when thinking about TTT, less is more. You are an English language teacher and you already know how to speak English, so after presentation, you can feel free to zip it. There are a couple principles behind TTT and why teachers should keep it to a minimum. I am sure you can think back to how boring it was to sit in a chair and listen to your previous teachers lecture for an hour, never engaging you as you slowly drifted into pleasant daydreams. This concept is universal and will happen to your students if a lecture ensues past the allocated T-ST talk time in your Presentation stage.

Usually, the time spent during the lesson is the only opportunity for your students to speak English to anyone, so let them have at it. You don't need to give up control of the classroom, but encourage a structured environment, following your PPP format that will allow your students plenty of time to speak English. This is a crucial and important part of English language teaching and should always be remembered before, during and after every lesson. Ask your students questions that will allow them to think about the lesson material in a focused manner and don't be so quick to give them the answers. Letting your students figure out things on their own will encourage them to speak more and could also lead into some group communication. Letting your students communicate in English is after all the whole purpose behind EFL and your student's overall language learning goals.

Creative Teacher Thinking

Following the PPP format when developing your lesson plan will allow you to note talk time as well as Teacher Talk Time (TTT).

With that said, how would you promote less TTT and more student communication? What can you do if you have a shy student?

Lesson Plan Format

Below is a general lesson plan format and would be how you would approach your lesson plan development. This outline can be used with any class size and is beneficial for you as a teacher to stay on track, have all teaching material ready and allow you to have confidence as you step into the classroom with a well thought out plan of action. Remember, share your aim and objectives with your students on the board, ensuring you both stay on track and reach the lesson aim in a timely and successful manner.

- ✓ **Lesson Name:**
- ✓ **Date and Time:**
- ✓ **Student Info and Level:** Age, English level, topics, any other student info.
- ✓ **Materials:** Everything and anything that you will need to teach the class and anything you need to bring to the lesson.
- ✓ **Textbook:** Name, chapter, page number.
- ✓ **Aim:** The goal for the lesson.
- ✓ **Objectives:** What is needed to accomplish the aim of the lesson?

- ✓ **Grammar:** The grammar points within the lesson if any.
- ✓ **Vocabulary:** The vocabulary within the lesson if any.
- ✓ **Questions and Answers:** Q and A related to the lesson, often asked in the warm-up.
- ✓ **Warm-up:** Brief discussion on the previous lesson, evoke conversation with Q and A format and get the communication flowing, relaxed and confident environment before beginning presentation.
- ✓ **Presentation:** Teacher time for introducing new material of the lesson, make it contextual and relevant.
- ✓ **Practice:** Allowing students to practice the new material, make sure to hover for corrections and on the spot teaching points.
- ✓ **Production:** Students take the floor and show what they have learned and practiced. TTT is limited, letting your students run with the new material in an exercise that is new and unrelated to the practice exercises.
- ✓ **Conclusion:** Wrap up the class with what was learned and see if the aim has been accomplished. Open the floor up for any questions and assign homework if needed.

An excellent thing to remember is to plan for possible interruptions or problems that may come up. It is always a good idea to think ahead about any possible scenarios that may arise, derailing the progress of the lesson. Another excellent habit to get into when developing your lesson plan using the lesson plan format is to note talking time and who should be talking somewhere in the plan to give a timeline to stick to, T-ST, PR or ST-ST.

Asking open ended questions is another way to ensure your creating a mentally creative classroom environment. Open ended questions cause your students to think harder and more insightfully, but in this, remember to stay silent a bit longer and allow time for your students to answer. Other helpful lesson hints are writing directions on the board and keep the classroom language calm and easy to understand. Being animated and using your non-verbal communication is great, but keeping the language simple will help your students hear you more clearly and remain focused on the task at hand.

Creative Teacher Thinking

It's time to make your first attempt at writing an effective lesson plan. Your student is a 45 year old professional who is taking private lessons with you on Monday evening at 6 pm after he gets off work. He is a pre-intermediate student and your last lesson discussed irregular verbs in past simple tense. Design your lesson plan using the above format and helpful hints and then go over the lesson plan checklist to see how you did.

Lesson Plan Checklist

1. I have taken the time to get to know my students and I am familiar with their native language, culture, habits, hobbies, work and English learning goals.

2. I have distinguished their English level and defined the areas important to develop lessons around.

3. I am aware of the time duration of the lesson.

4. I have created a lesson topic that can be expressed contextually and is relevant.

5. I have set a clear aim and objectives for the lesson.

6. I have looked over my lesson for any problems that may arise during the lesson.

7. I have obtained all the material I need to teach this lesson effectively.

8. I understand the ins and outs of the new material and know fully what I need to present to the students.

9. I have a controlled practice exercise prepared for the students after presentation.

10. I have developed an exercise for free student practice after the controlled practice has been completed.

11. I have ensured my lesson has plenty of ST-ST, PR and GR talk time to let the students communicate effectively.

12. I have developed a production exercise that will allow the students to clearly show what they have learned and practiced in the lesson.

13. I have noted time increments, T-ST and TTT in my lesson plan and TTT is appropriate with the lesson format.

Chapter Four

Presentation Teaching Material

Chapter Overview:

Presentation Stage

Questions that Develop Answers

Creating a Visual Presentation

Showing Time as Linear

Board Work

Checking Student Competency

Presentation Stage

We discussed Presentation, Practice, and Production (PPP) in the last chapter and went over each part in brief detail so you can visualize how to begin developing your own lesson plans. In this chapter we will be focusing on Presentation, the actual teaching stage of the lesson, so get your note taking material ready, this stuff is important. Presentation is the first main part of the lesson, often after review and warm-up, presentation time is the time for the teacher to show his or her stuff and begin introducing new material their students. As we discussed previously, this is the shortest section of the PPP format and after Presentation, TTT should be at a minimum. Keep a creative mind when developing your Presentation and always remember, keep it relevant, useful and contextual.

Questions that Develop Answers

No student enjoys a lecture, the traditional method of a teacher standing in front of the class and giving information with little to no student participation. This is the class environment that evokes boredom and lack of interest and enthusiasm by students. The key to a successful, communicative and informative lesson is to ask questions and evoke student participation. In the world of English language learning, all students have one simple and universal goal behind the countless hours of English class, they want to be able to communicate in English! By asking questions and pulling those answers out of your students, you are creating an open environment where they are able to speak English with you and other students.

Another factor behind the use of questions during presentation is that it also allows your student to start thinking, processing and developing answers in English. Most daily life is surrounded by questions and we must process and develop solutions for these questions in a timely manner in order to move forward in our day. It is the same for your students in their native language, but now is the time for them to begin mentally processing in English faster and more clearly. Engage your students and they will engage you back.

Here are a few positive key aspects behind using questions during the Presentation stage of your well planned lesson. Always asking questions will eliminate most boredom and allow your students to stay actively in the classroom, not daydreaming about the weekend. Your students will also be sitting at the edge of their seats in anticipation for what question might be coming next and they will most certainly be waiting to have their chance to answer and communicate in English. Using questions will also allow your students to develop a process to work out a response to your answer using English. Instead of listening to you tell them what the answers are, they have to guess and figure it out on their own.

Feedback and checking how much your student's are retaining is also another benefit to asking questions during presentation. If they listen to a lecture, it may go in one ear and out the other, leaving problems in the Practice stage since they may not fully understand what the new material represents. Questions will allow you as a teacher to check in with your students and see if they really grasp the material. Also, if they know they may be called upon to answer something, they might pay more attention in fear of possible embarrassment if they do not know the answer. Lastly, asking your students questions will eliminate unnecessary Teacher Talk Time (TTT). Keeping your students talking and thinking in English will benefit their learning goals and they will appreciate the time they have to communicate in the language they are so excited to learn. Though the benefits of using questions in your Presentation are more abundant than the negatives, there are still negatives to the process. It is important to understand when to ask a question, how often and what kind of question you should ask. If you ask too many questions and if your scaling is not appropriate, your students can become irritated and shut down. Keep the questions short, concise and at a good tempo. Another downfall to using questions is that it can produce answers from only a few eager students. Pay close attention to this scenario and if you identify it early enough, you can address this possible issue and get more students involved, participating and communicating. This could be a great note in your lesson plan format, identifying possible problems during the lesson and how to overcome the problems in appositive way.

Creative Teacher Thinking

In a Presentation on irregular verbs, what would be some excellent questions to ask in order to promote interest and communication? Remember, your questions should be short, concise and keep the question relevant to the specific answer you want. You can use leading questions to help progress the lesson in your desired direction. You still have control of the classroom and lesson with TTT.

Creating a Visual Presentation

The use of visual stimulants in your Presentation is an extremely important practice for you as a teacher to get familiar with. Again, English language teaching methods differ from the traditional lecture and basic content associated with other educational courses. English teachers possess a wide variety of visual aids that stimulate their student's imaginations, creating a fire storm of enthusiasm within the classroom. Using pictures, videos or other visual aids can help you establish the attention needed to successfully introduce new material to your students in a way they will be eager to understand and often boosts material retention. Don't forget, when introducing new material, it is important to start with something familiar and work your way forward from there. Utilizing visual stimulants can help make that familiar object or content more real and will help you set up a solid foundation for the introduction of your new material, often related to the familiar object.

A great example of this is a lesson which expands vocabulary surrounding food and dining. If your students are Japanese, you can start with a picture of sushi, since almost everyone in Japan and around the world is familiar with the word and picture of sushi. From this point you have connected and can begin introducing new relevant material. This can be accomplished by showing your students a picture of a plate of sushi, on a table, with a green table cloth, chopsticks, napkin, fork, knife, glass and so on. You can see how a familiar picture and word can be expanded into a wide variety of vocabulary. This can also be paired with questions of course, creating creative answers that provoke communication in English.

Visual stimulation can come in all shapes and sizes. Pictures of real life scenarios or more simple photos depending on the student's level are great. Short video clips are also useful, but always remember time and make sure the video clips are not too long, you still want to promote student speaking time. Slide shows, hand crafted power point presentations are also great ways to deliver your visual material, keeping it organized, easy to see and accessible by the student after the lesson is over. You have the power as an English language teacher to get creative with your visual aids and it is a good idea to compile a large variety of visual aids in order to have the ability to choose at will, depending on the lesson and situation.

Creative Teacher Thinking

What visual aids would you use when presenting clothing vocabulary to your pre-intermediate students? What Questions could you ask to elicit answers and student communication? How long should your Presentation be if your lesson time is one hour?

Showing Time as Linear

Along the lines of visual aids and helping your students understand new material in a way that is more visual and interesting, showing time in a linear way can be beneficial for your students. During the course of many lessons, time and the various tenses within the material will be introduced, explained, reintroduced and you can complement words with a simple visual aid. You can complement any tense discussion by drawing a line and labeling areas along the line as they correspond with past, present and future. For example, if you are discussing something in the past simple tense, you could make a mark on the line that the student can associate with past simple.

Board Work

In our previous section discussing the use of a linear timeline to give a more visual appearance to tenses, it is important that you understand board work and the use of the chalkboard or whiteboard, whichever you have in your classroom. You may think that using the chalkboard or whiteboard is pretty straightforward, but it is important to understand and be ready when using one during class. The most important part associated with board work is organization. Just as your lesson plan should be organized and understandable, the same applies for your board work. Students find a messy board distracting and can be somewhat irritating when trying to piece together the notes they took during a messy board work lesson.

I had a professor in university that had horrible board work habits and it caused my notes to mirror his board work notes. Keep it organized, keep it in categories and get rid of what is not needed as you progress through your lesson. Here are a few simple concepts to begin practicing before approaching the board during your class. Keep your writing legible and in a straight line so there is no mistake about what is important and where it falls within the notes. Along with straight lines and legible handwriting comes categories. When you are developing your lesson plan, take a few minutes and think about how you could categorize the material in a clear way when doing board work (if applicable).

This should go without saying, but as an English language teacher, you shouldn't have ANY spelling mistakes in your board work. Stay professional during your board work and you won't have students asking why you spelt a word wrong if they catch your mistake. Lastly, using different colored markers will also help break up note sections and keep things organized, just make sure all your markers are working correctly and that you have erasable markers, not permanent, it happens sometimes. Use that board to your advantage; it can help you produce charts, graphs and other visual aids to assist in your Presentation of new material.

As the world gets smaller and smaller through the use of computers and technological advances, many of your students might meet you in the virtual classroom. Online lessons are becoming more and more popular since adult students are getting less personal time and often time spent commuting to a language school is seen as time wasted. Many students are enjoying the comfortable setting of online language classes. There is no commuting, they are at home and relaxed and they can get one on one access to a teacher instead of sitting in a class, competing for a teacher's attention.

If this is the case, it is important that you are completely familiar with the messaging or chat-box system of whatever online program you are using for your lesson. Nowadays, most class are taught via Skype, so get familiar with messaging, sharing screens and know that students often use their messenger as their notes and will appreciate you writing all new words and answers to any questions they may have for you.

Creative Teacher Thinking

As discussed, board work is important and understanding the importance of effective board work is essential to your teacher skills. What is the most important rule behind board work? How can you organize your board work when writing notes on past simple tense questions and answers? For example: What did you do last week (question)? Last week I worked and watched a lot of TV after work (answer). How could you organize similar questions and answers while also using a timeline to illustrate past simple tense?

Checking Student Competency

Your student's understanding of the new material is extremely important and it is essential that you check their competency before moving into the Practice stage of the PPP format. If students do not fully understand the new material, the Practice stage is really a waste of time since they can't Practice what they do not know. There are a few different ways to check your student's competency and if you have been asking a lot of concise questions throughout the Presentation stage, you are already getting an idea of who gets it and who doesn't. One ineffective way of checking competency is to ask your students if they understand, "do you understand?" This question accomplishes nothing, because maybe they do, but maybe they have no idea what is going on and they just say yes to avoid embarrassment or to keep the class moving because they are bored. When checking competency, get your students involved, just like every part of the English language process, communication is key.

Some good methods to this concept are multiple choice questions, creating a response from your students that can only represent new material understanding. Yes and No answer questions are also good when time is running low or the content is not that in depth. Another interesting method to checking competency is to have your students answer with action. Let's say you were discussing actions relating to clothing, you can ask your elementary student, "How do you brush your teeth?" This will cause them to complete an action that represents the answer. Lastly, open ended questions are also good ways to see if your students are fully engaged in the new material. Again, focusing on student talk time is important and making sure your students are confident and understand the material will save you time and energy during the Practice stage of your well planned lesson.

Creative Teacher Thinking

Why is checking your student's understanding of the new material introduced in the Presentation stage? How would you check competency for students learning about comparatives and superlatives?

Chapter Five

Presentation and Vocabulary

Chapter Overview:

Vocabulary Building

Vocabulary Functionality

What does it Really Mean?

Putting Words Together

Grammar Building in Presentation

Vocabulary Building in Presentation

Before you begin developing your lesson plan on vocabulary, it's important to first think about how you learn new words. In your daily life, if you come across a new word, where do you go to research it? What information do you get when you research it? What part of that information is useful to you for really understanding that new word? These are all excellent questions to think about when discussing the topic of presenting vocabulary to your students. In today's technological world, most of us and our students will do an internet search in order to discover the meaning of a new word, words and/or phrases. When you get the results of your web search, you normally only get one, maybe two definitions with some popular synonyms and maybe one example as well. This is normally sufficient to get the general meaning of a new word, but as English language teachers, it may be beneficial to go a bit further in our Presentation.

When thinking about presenting new vocabulary to your students, these are some important aspects that will assist you in successfully explaining the new material to your students that will create competency and communication. First off, we need the meaning of the new vocabulary word in all its relevant forms. There is no need to confuse students with definitions to new words that are never used in that definitions context anymore. Always remember to keep things relevant and in saying that, make sure the synonyms and antonyms you choose to present with the word are also commonly used. If your students are not studying for a post graduate entrance exam, than don't introduce confusing, uncommon words on top of new vocabulary.

Other important aspects surrounding vocabulary presentation to consider are spelling, pronunciation, connotation, collocation, register, syntax, word family, visuals and parts of speech. It is not always relevant to address all the many aspects surrounding a new vocabulary word. Often, it is enough to cover the basic elements and what needs to be known in order to get your intended objective across and successfully achieve your aim. The outline for presenting vocabulary is solely up to the teacher to decide when you are developing a quality lesson plan and presenting new vocabulary to your students. For example, you can see a few relevant aspects surrounding the word "carry." This can be written on the board to illustrate for notes and can also be paired with photos and slides for visual connection with the definitions. Sometimes your new vocabulary will have popular phrases, phrasal verbs and/or idioms associated with them, so depending on your student's level; you can incorporate it into your vocabulary presentation.

Here is a great example for vocabulary building using the word carry:

- √ **Definition 1:** Support and move someone or something from one place to another.
- √ **Example 1:** He had to carry the box down the stairs by himself.
- √ **Definition 2:** Support the weight of.
- √ **Example 1:** The bridge can carry heavy loads.
- √ **Definition 3:** To transmit, transport or conduct.
- √ **Example 3:** Someone can carry a disease and transmit it to others.

- ✓ **Synonyms:** Bring, lift, move, take, tote, haul…
- ✓ **Antonyms:** Drop, keep, lower, stay, remain…
- ✓ **Word Families:** Carry, carrying, carried, carries (verb). Carries (noun).
- ✓ **Phrases:** Carry conviction, carry the weight.
- ✓ **Phrasal Verbs:** Get carried away, carry on.

With your new vocabulary word defined and ready for presentation, you can now begin constructing the outline of the lesson. Like your lesson plan, being an English language teacher is all about being prepared and developing outlines and plans that will ensure class success. The important elements to define are class, student English level, materials needed for instruction, any problems involved and of course your lesson aims and objectives to keep you and your students on track during class.

Here are a few sample ideas on how we can present the word carry and the order in which you can present your new material to your class:

1. Start with the basics, showing photos of people carrying things, maybe even a funny video if you can find one on the internet. Ask your students what these people are carrying, why and so on. Have your students write their thoughts and ideas down.

2. Involve your students in peer communication and have them write what each person was carrying below the organized sections for each photo on the board.

3. Next, introduce some other, more challenging definitions involved with the verb carry. A good way to do this would be to show a photo of a pregnant woman and ask the students what they see and then ask if the woman is carrying anything. This should create communication and enthusiasm to find out what she is carrying.

4. Once all relevant and common use definitions are explained using visual aids and communication, you can move into opposites and similar words (synonyms and antonyms).

5. Divide the verb and noun form to explain each word family.

6. Check competency with concept questions.

There are of course many other ideas and parts you can add to this presentation, but you can see a basic formula that will help you give a great presentation to your students using visual aids and communication.

Creative Teacher Thinking

The previous section discussed vocabulary presentation and some important key points to address when presenting new vocabulary to your eager students. Think about land features and the many different vocabulary words that can be found in one landscape photo. You can find hills, mountains, valleys, ridges, plateaus, rivers, and so on. How could you develop a vocabulary presentation about land features? What is important to include? What visual aids and material would be useful?

Vocabulary Functionality

Presenting new vocabulary to your students often comes with a lot of explanation and examples about the meaning of the words and the way they are used in sentences, conversation and/or life. The way we use words refers to the function of a word and it is important to share the function of new words in a relevant way that the students will remember and be able to use in the future. Functionality lessons revolve around the context or the setting of a situation prior to the presentation of new material, for example new vocabulary. In our vocabulary presentation example we used the word carry and in functionality teaching, you would present a situation where carrying is used often. An excellent example for the word carry would be a shopping mall scenario.

People are carrying all types of things in a shopping mall and you can use this function to present your new vocabulary in all its different forms, as well as in phrases and phrasal verbs, depending on student level. Using a functional approach, you can show your students how to use new vocabulary in real world situations that they will most certainly experience. Everyone goes to the shopping mall or something similar, a market perhaps, and you can not only develop a lesson around new vocabulary, but around functionality in a situation they will encounter.

A few examples surrounding functionality teaching within a context while presenting new vocabulary:

- ✓ What time are we meeting at the mall today?
- ✓ What stores should we go to?
- ✓ Can you carry my bags while I call my mom to pick us up?
- ✓ I think my favorite store is carrying the new perfume I want to try.

What Does It Really Mean?

Words have all sorts of definitions and meanings, so it is important to explain to your students the connotations associated with the new vocabulary you are presenting to them. The worst thing that can happen to your students is that they use a word in the wrong connotation and cause them to feel embarrassed or it could also get them into some trouble depending on the word and connotation.

Understanding connotation is important and can allow your students to understand when and where to use a word properly and it will help them avoid embarrassment or a possible blow to their English speaking confidence. Another important aspect involved with word connotation is whether a word is positive, negative and/or neutral. Some words can be all three depending on the situation and that is why explaining connotation to your students is so important.

Creative Teacher Thinking

Connotation is important and one area where connotation could be used in the wrong way is body description of others. There are various ways to describe someone's body type, many positive, negative and/or neutral words can be used in this particular situation. What are some examples of positive, negative and neutral body types that could be useful for your students to know?

Putting Words Together

Putting words together is the cornerstone to native speech and understanding vocabulary in this sense can allow your students to see the bigger picture behind vocabulary and structure. Words that often go together are defined as collocations and they are extremely useful for your students when analyzing new words and it can give you the teacher a chance to present your new vocabulary in groups.

Collocations is a little different than the previous example discussing landscape features, even though each landscape word is considered to belong to a specific group, the individual words do not pair together in a sentence structure. Collocations go deeper into word pairs and can be presented in forms like subject + verb, verb + object, adjective + noun. Give your students the opportunity to figure out these word groups by asking what word comes after what in example questions and you can also make them come up with their own questions while discussing it with their peers.

Another excellent way to present vocabulary is using the opposite formula of the main words you are presenting. We discussed synonyms and antonyms previously, but this goes a little deeper and yet it is more simplistic. Pairing or grouping your new vocabulary with similar and opposite words will add weight to what your students are learning and they will have a more whole understanding. Always remember to do your competency checks before moving on to the Practice stage, ensuring all your students are moving in the right direction.

Creative Teacher Thinking

What would be ten excellent new vocabulary words with their designated antonyms and synonyms? How could you present these words? Remember to choose only one word for the antonym and synonym, the most commonly used of course, to ensure a quality understanding without cluttering the new vocabulary.

Grammar Building in Presentation

Presenting grammar during your lesson can be fun and if your lesson plan is developed appropriately, can engage your students in a very lively and enthusiastic discussion. The format for presenting grammar is similar to presenting vocabulary; only the material and aims differ. You still need to know your students, their English levels, the materials you need to give quality instruction, define any problems, and set your aims and objectives. When presenting grammar, you can often involve one of the various tenses during your presentation, depending on the level of your students of course. You will still use several visual aids and examples to illustrate the new grammar content, show the different forms (positive, negative, question form), make sure pronunciation and structure is noted of course, show function and of course check for student competency throughout and at the end of your new grammar presentation.

Creative Teacher Thinking

Following the outline for presenting vocabulary, think of a good presentation approach for a grammar lesson. Your class is a private class, the student is at a pre-intermediate level, your material will be photos and examples. What are your aims and objectives? What will you present for this English level?

Chapter Six

Practice and Organization

Chapter Overview:

Use for New Vocabulary

Benefits of Practice

Presentation to Practice

Pair Practice

Group Practice

Use for New Vocabulary

In chapters four and five, we discussed the presentation stage of our teaching format, Presentation, Practice and Production (PPP). We discussed some excellent ways to present new vocabulary and also compared it with new grammar presentation as well. It is always important to remember the time requirements that are categorized in the PPP format when developing your lesson plan. The Presentation stage consumes the least amount of time in your lesson, moving on after you ensure the competency level is satisfactory, your next lesson stage is Practice. In this chapter we will address the key aspects involved with the Practice stage and you will gain knowledge in developing a few excellent Practice methods and techniques.

During your Presentation of new material, vocabulary or grammar, the Teacher Talk Time (TTT) was at its highest point of the lesson and it involves mainly T -ST discussion with a little room if applicable for ST - ST discussion. The Practice stage will limit your T - ST to "only when necessary" as you let the students practice and participate in more ST - ST talk time during controlled practice exercises. The key word in the Practice stage is "controlled" and is very important to remember when developing exercises for your students to work on. Controlled practice will allow your student to practice, of course, what they learned during the presentation stage in a controlled, focused and somewhat predictable manner. You want your students to become completely comfortable and confident with the new material during the practice stage in order to make for a smooth transition into the Production stage. You want to develop exercises that will keep your student's focus on the new material alone, not letting them run with all the new knowledge they have quite yet.

Creative Teacher Thinking

In review, why is it important to limit TTT during the presentation stage? Why is the TTT so low during a lesson? Where do you note the expected talking times and lesson development times and why is it a good practice to do this?

Benefits of Practice

Practice exercises serve various purposes and will allow your student to really build confidence and deep understanding of the material you presented so perfectly in the Presentation stage. Your Practice exercises should focus on accuracy and should allow your students to predict the answers using the new material only, but remember to make it somewhat challenging. Also, it is always good to remember scaling, making each exercise a bit more challenging than the previous one. Don't just use one example for an exercise, get creative in your question choices to keep the student guessing, but in a predictable way. Repetition and making your questions only answerable if they truly understand the material is also important to keep in mind when designing your Practice exercises.

Here is a great example of challenging yet predictable practice questions that are fill in the blank:

Put the verb into Present Continuous form and complete the sentence.
Example: When **is** she **coming** home? (come)

1. They _____ _____ their books. (read)

2. Is he _____ or _____ ? (sit, stand)

3. What _____ you _____ tonight? (do)

4. I ____ _____ to become a lawyer. (study)

You can see how each question is a bit more challenging than the one before, not by a lot, but it does force the student to think about the new material, focus on that particular area (present continuous) and fill in the gap appropriately. If your students did not have the proper understanding of the new material, it would be obvious in their answers to the questions. These types of practice exercises are also excellent competency checks as well.

Using these types of exercises in the Practice stage are also excellent ways to create mental muscle memory through repetition. Your students can focus on the new material without distraction, over and over, creating positive and confident results over and over again as well. These exercises also promote confidence as they develop more structured and controlled understanding of the new material through repetition in their practice.

Design your exercise in ways that give your students sufficient practice as you maintain classroom control. They will enjoy the ST - ST talk time as they compare and discuss the answers together, but there is also an alternative motive behind your controlled practice.

You will have the freedom to move around the classroom and listen into what your students are discussing. This will allow you to do on the spot corrections and check your student's competency without TTT getting in the way. Another excellent habit to get into during the Practice stage is having a Practice stage wrap up. Make sure your students give quality feedback and you can take that opportunity to answer any questions and correct any problems that arise before moving on to the Production stage.

Creative Teacher Thinking

Thinking about the Practice exercise example in this section, why is it important for the exercise to be focused on the new material only? How could you develop a controlled Practice exercise surrounding new vocabulary or grammar material discussing the present perfect tense?

Presentation to Practice

During your Presentation of new material, you were utilizing TTT and giving T - ST instruction as you presented new material to your students. The transition in the Practice stage can be easily formatted at the end of your presentation and your students won't even realize they had moved into the next stage of the lesson. This is good practice for your lesson flow and it keeps the class engagement moving forward without delays or pauses that can often derail attention from material. While engaging your class in concept questions, checking competency of the new material, you can slyly transition from competency questions within your Presentation wrap up to controlled classroom practice.

Engaging all the students of the class at the first point of entering the Practice stage, you can answer questions and correct any issues for the benefit of the whole class. When teaching English as a foreign language, or teaching in general, you will always come across students that remain silent and go through the motions, possibly without fully understanding parts of the material. Engaging the whole class with positive encouragement will bring some of those questions to light and give your shy students the information they needed without them asking. This of course is not the best practice, but it is an excellent technique to combat your future shy students. This moment can also allow you to cover anything that may have slipped off the lesson plan and also give your students even more confidence and practice before moving into the next section of the Practice stage.

Control is important during Practice and there is a method to slowly releasing control little by little to your students as you approach PR - PR talk time, putting students in pairs to Practice the new material. A good technique to get groups moving in the right direction is to pair everyone up and then you join each pair as a mediator between the students and the practice exercise you have developed for the new material. This still keeps you in control while also keeping the whole class engaged while they are in their pairs. For example, with the whole class engaged in your instruction, pick a group and begin the exercise.

Past Simple Exercise (Irregular Verbs):

- ✓ "Tim and Mary, what did each of you eat for dinner last night?" (Teacher)
- ✓ "I ate spaghetti." (Tim)
- ✓ "I ate mac and cheese." (Mary)
- ✓ "Excellent, ate is the past simple tense for eat." (Teacher)

In this example, the whole class listens to the answers and if there is something out of place in either of their answers, you can ask them to think about it for a second and retry. This engages the pair and the whole class as you keep control of the lesson and the first pair Practice. You can use the board and write your exercise questions or a good idea would be a visual aid here as well.

After a round with each pair, turn it over to them as they ask and answer each other, one at a time, in front of the whole class. Still in control and listening to them as they answer, only allow yourself to intervene to make a correction or give positive encouragement. TTT should slowly decline here as the students move forward into working alone in pairs without the whole class engaged.

Creative Teacher Thinking

Why is it important to remain control during the Practice stage? What is a good way for you to transition from Presentation to Practice? Can you write out a detailed example of how you would transition from Presentation to Practice while keeping control and your class engaged?

Pair Practice

In order for practice exercise to be effective, you need to give your students the ability to visualize and understand the new material, rules, and/or structure that surrounds the new material that they learned in your amazing Presentation. There are several techniques, exercises and methods for your students to fully understand the new material during the controlled Practice stage and all these exercises will consist of reading, writing and listening.

Here are a few excellent examples for Practice:

1. Matching exercises are of course the textbook standard for learning exercises and we have all experienced doing these in our young academic years. You can match furniture with rooms in a home or match verbs with activities.

Bed	**Kitchen**
Television	**Bedroom**
Shower	**Family Room**
Fridge	**Bathroom**

2. Another great exercise for Practice is anagrams and it can be paired with sentence construction after the word is realized.

M(tiouann)   Mountain   I live near a mountain (student sentence construction)

R(evri)

yevall

3. Using text and having the students underline words can be used in several different ways and is a good way to get your students reading and communicating with each other as they try to identify the words and their relation to the new material. For example, text with past continuous words can be spotted and underlined by the students and

they can compare their answers or do the exercise as a team. Another text exercise could allow your student to define the underlined words and write or communicate the synonyms or antonyms of the new vocabulary they learned during Presentation.

4. Piecing together sentences that have been scrambled into a mess is also a fun activity for your students as they work in pairs. They can work together to solve the problem and use critical thinking of what they know to piece the sentence back together properly.

Communication is extremely important when your students are working in pairs and as an English language teacher, you have two main objectives during the Practice stage. Firstly, get them engaged and focused on the material so their understanding can grow with their confidence as they work together. Secondly, getting your students to communicate with each other is the cornerstone of why they are learning English in the first place.

An effective way to get your students involved with one another is developing a script of questions and answers or some other material that encompasses the new material that allows them to communicate in a contextual way. Visual aids can also be used by your students as they ask each other to describe what they see and they can even get creative in their communication as long as it stays on topic. Your movement around the room will allow you to pick up on any issues and bring any important teaching notes to the attention of the class.

Group Practice

Group practice is also a great way to get more students engaged and can often build team building and confidence within your students. Group Practice brings the class together and it can also add some competition between groups that can be fun and exciting before moving into the Production stage. You can do some research and find many great group exercises to implement into your Practice lesson plan.

- ✓ Trivia questions revolving around new vocabulary is a great way to get groups to engage in communication and practice the new material. You can give small hints and each group must try to figure out which new vocabulary word the hints correspond to.

- ✓ Another great group exercise is to place a small text in one corner of the room and have members of each group spend 30 seconds looking at the text and bringing back the information orally to their group members to write it down on paper. At the end of the exercise, the group with the closest dictation of the text wins. Having rewards is optional for the groups and it is best to always reward the whole class regardless of who wins.

These are just a few examples of exceptional pair and group exercises you can use in your Practice stage with your eager students. Remember to maintain control as you let your students practice more and more as the lesson progresses. Let them communicate with one another as TTT goes down and ST talk time goes up. Control, material focus and communication are the most important factors to an excellent Practice stage within your lesson.

Creative Teacher Thinking

What are the three most important areas to think about when developing and implementing your Practice exercises? Thinking about pair exercises, what would your Practice plan be for your elementary students who had a Presentation on weather vocabulary? What would your group Practice exercise be relating to the same Presentation?

Chapter Seven

Production and Organization

Chapter Overview:

Production Concepts

Production Ideas

Implementing an Exercise

Organizing Students

The New Material Trifecta

Production Concepts

The Production stage is where it all comes together for your student and if everything goes as planned. A great Presentation and effective Practice, your student will be able to use the new language effectively. Here you want your student to take all the target language that he confidently built and use it in a natural way, in a suitable setting. Your exercises should allow your students to utilize either speaking or writing to convey their knowledge of the new material with little to no assistance from you, the teacher.

Production Ideas

One easy production exercise that we are all familiar with is a writing exercise involving the new material. Above all, you want your students to become creative and enthusiastic in their Production exercise, so though a writing exercise is effective, it might lack some enthusiasm from your student. Writing exercises do come with some extra help from the teacher and it is always a good idea to go over structure of the writing assignment with your student. Give them an example format and make it accessible as they create their masterpiece that includes all the new material they have spent all lesson learning and practicing. Combining a writing exercise with a presentation is always a good idea and will encourage communication and confident speaking skills.

Another effective exercise that can be used in the Production stage comes back to PR - PR talk time, putting your students back into pairs or transitioning from Practice to Production while they are still in their existing pairs. In the Practice stage you could have them read a script back and forth to one another with the focus of the script being on the new material. This exercise can be reshaped a bit for the Production stage, where you make them create their own script with the new material and then discussing it with their partner.

Creating interviews and having teammates interview each other is a great way for your class to learn about their fellow classmates as well as promote communication and facilitate Production of the material. Again, it is important to show your students an interview structure and have it available for them to reference as they create their interview questions. Creativity is an important aspect to Production and a good structure with example formats is just as important for their growth.

Group exercises in the Production stage are always great for class growth, camaraderie and will influence a flow of communication as they let their creativity take over. One well known and widely used Production exercise is the creation of a play. This gets the whole class involved and you can incorporate individual roles for each student. For example, if the new material is clothing or shopping, the setting could be a busy store in a shopping center and each student will have a role to play within the store. Give out characters, but not a script. One can be the store associate, one an angry customer and so on. They can develop their characters and decide what lines they will say and when. It is a fun exercise that can really allow them to use their new language in a context not too far off from real life.

Creative Teacher Thinking

In the Production stage, what would you like your student to be able to do? Why? Can you describe a Production exercise that would be effective for pre-intermediate students that have had a Presentation in different parts of the human body?

Implementing an Exercise

The cornerstone of a successful, amazing Production exercise or any part of your lesson is the way you implement your instructions for that particular exercise. If your instructions and examples are not the best, then of course, your student's understanding and/or progress will reflect that. Always remember who you are talking to, what level, what type of class and so on. It is easy for teachers to get lost in the material and begin rambling faster and faster as the lesson progresses. Stay confident and relaxed as you deliver your instruction clearly, in short sentences and in a dialogue fitting for the English level.

If one thing has become more and more prevalent in this text, is that proper and adequate planning is essential in English language teaching. Write out your instructions for yourself first, whether in your lesson plan or on a paper that compliments your lesson plan. This will allow you to take a good look at it and format in a way that will be concise and help you deliver the instructions in a step by step format that is easy for anyone to understand.

Think of it like you are putting together some piece of furniture you recently bought. How would you want to be instructed? Again, the use of visuals is also an exceptional way to get your instructions across in a clear and easy to understand way. Keep these visuals and examples in sight or accessible for your students to refer to later in the lesson, which will help keep the lesson flow moving in the right direction and also allow you to stay on track.

Creative Teacher Thinking

What are the three key components behind giving exceptional instructions for your students to complete an exercise successfully? Why is thinking about giving instructions important for a teacher?

Organizing Students

Something so simple is often very important and organizing your students in an effective way is one of those simple tasks that can have negative implications if not done correctly. One major aspect of proper organization is making sure that your pairs and groups are in the same level and can communicate and understand effectively as a team. You don't want imbalance if it can be avoided, but unfortunately this will happen and it is part of the English language teaching environment. Do your best at getting your groups and pairs organized by level or getting it as close as possible.

Another important component to remember when organizing your class into pairs and groups is to maintain control in the process. Do not let them put themselves in pairs or groups; there are too many moving parts to be considered. Use body language and polite hand movements to gesture to your students that they are now a pair or this half of the class is now a group. Avoid pointing, numbering, lettering or anything that might be seen as rude or even misunderstood as you organize them. This can be a fun exercise in itself and you can brainstorm and implement some fun ways to organize the class and encourage communication in the process.

Creative Teacher Thinking

Why is organizing your class correctly so important? Describe a creative way you can organize your class for a pair and group exercise?

The New Material Trifecta

When discussing Presentation, Practice and Production (PPP), we have gone over and seen a few great examples for you to utilize as an English language teacher. Putting together a well-developed lesson plan that flows is important and there is an element to this that can be useful in your PPP format. With a little research and teacher creativity, you can develop a Presentation, Practice and Production lesson that is all about one single topic. For example, you can present a short paragraph about global warming to your students and then discuss the verbs and tenses within the text during the Presentation stage.

Using this same material, focus your Practice around those very same verbs and tenses while using similar context about global warming in the exercises. Lastly, let your students get creative and have them write and present their own thoughts on global warming and what actions might be beneficial to help the environment. You can see how one piece of material can be used throughout the entire PPP lesson and it will allow for a forward flowing class that is organized and focused the entire time. This method takes a little creativity, but is often a successful way to engage your students in communication and increase understanding of the new material.

Creative Teacher Thinking

When thinking about lesson flow and creating a PPP that covers a single topic, how could this be beneficial for you as a teacher and your students? Briefly outline a PPP lesson that covers one topic while creating a quality foundation for your new material.

Chapter Eight

Giving Corrections and Allowing Feedback

Chapter Overview:

Organizing Mistakes

Accuracy and Fluency

Body Language

Encourage Self-Correction

Student to Student Correction

Feedback Essentials

Writing Corrections

Correcting within Structure

Testing

Organizing Mistakes

In the world of English language learning and teaching, mistakes are a daily occurrence and become commonplace whether the mistakes are worth discussing or not. Many teachers struggle with a few elements when it comes to making corrections. Some feel that on the spot corrections are best, while others feel that on the spot corrections could be considered rude and could diminish a student's confidence. These teachers take a more polite approach, correcting students after the fact, allowing them to continue in the exercise. In native English there are many mistakes in a conversation between native speakers and in these situations, mistakes are often ignored as the conversation continues on and on.

Unfortunately, there is no right or wrong way to correct students, no one step outline that will allow you to be more efficient in your corrections and feedback. You may have students who prefer on the spot corrections and other students who feel that is to forward or harsh and prefer a more sensitive approach. However, one thing remains as the cornerstone to corrections and feedback, you are a teacher and that is one of the most important aspects of the profession. Without corrections and positive feedback, students form poor speaking, writing and/or reading habits that will only harm progress in the long run. As a teacher, giving exceptional corrections and positive feedback will keep your students moving forward with confidence and enthusiasm to continue learning English.

Here are the major issues regarding corrections and some essential points to remember when addressing them:

When dealing with corrections, one common problem is knowing when to correct and this often proves to be a tricky task. Another important aspect to consider is defining the grey area within accuracy and fluency. Also knowing the specific errors to correct and how to approach those corrections, for example what method to use to correct, are also very important key aspects when discussing corrections.

With the above in mind, let's discuss some helpful guidelines to keep in your teacher tool kit when approaching corrections. The grey area or balance between accuracy and fluency is one of the most important to ponder, since accuracy in the subject can directly influence fluency. Also, if the student is exhibiting a good form of communication, the correction can often come later, but if communication is slow and declining, it is a good idea to jump in and get the student back on track. Another aspect of communication is a total pause in it, due to an error in the subject material by the student. If communication comes to a dead halt, than jump in and put extreme importance on the correction to get communication flowing again.

✓ Define if accuracy is interfering with fluency.
✓ Let correction wait if communication is flowing and good.
✓ Step in immediately and discuss corrections if communication stops al together.

Creative Teacher Thinking

We discussed some common problems you may face as an English language teacher in regards to corrections and feedback. What are a few of those issues when discussing corrections? What are the three aspects of quality correction and why are they useful?

Accuracy and Fluency

When wrapping your head around accuracy and fluency, just remember one thing, if the student makes a minor slip, wait and see where it goes before jumping in. A good example of this is when your student is delivering his paragraph verbally on a task that revolves around the past simple.

Maria: When I was 10 years old, **I go** to the beach where my family and I played in the ocean and on the beach. I enjoyed the beach very much and we went many times after that.

In the sentences above, you can note that Maria made a mistake in the beginning of her speech about the beach. She said "I go" instead of "I went," but the rest of her speech was correct, so letting her continue enabled her to establish **fluency** with a minor **accuracy** error. Stopping her immediately could have caused some confidence decline, so it is always good to see where it goes, make a note of it and address it after her fluency is completed. However, if she went on to make another accuracy mistake that could be a good indicator that the material was not understood fully and correction should be implemented at that point.

If the student is still communicating well and fluency is good with a minor accuracy error, make notes and wait, but if communication is in decline, jump in and do some competency checks regarding the new material. One aspect surrounding this example is also what type of correction is needed by you the teacher. If the mistake is a minor mistake due to nervousness or just a good old fashion slip up, you can just point it out and the student will immediately understand the mistake and how to correct it themselves. However, if the mistake results in a decline of accuracy and communication, a more detailed explanation is better, giving the students a more well-rounded perspective of the mistake and the correct way to use the new material. This will keep confidence and accuracy high as they feel more relaxed when receiving positive feedback and corrections.

Creative Teacher Thinking

What are the important things to remember when discussing accuracy and fluency? If a student makes a minor mistake in accuracy when doing a Production exercise, what action would you take? If a student makes a major mistake, what action would you take?

Useful Body Language

We all have specific body language movements that are unique to our personality and we can use this body language to our teaching advantage when giving a Presentation on new material as well as when you give corrections and feedback. Your students will actually become tuned into tour specific body language since they will spend a lot of their time in class watching you move around as you speak. Utilize your body language to animate your teaching and give quality corrections to your eager and attentive students. You can also combine your body language with voice tone when delivering corrections to your students, driving home the point and allowing them to also think actively about the mistake and correction.

Here are a few great body language techniques for correction:

✓ **Tenses.** When discussing tenses, something that may be confusing to your early level students, use your hands, fingers and gestures to put it into their learning muscle memory. Point backwards for past, forward for future and down to represent the present, the here and now. This creates an impactful way for them to always remember and some of them will begin doing the same hand gestures when describing tense to classmates or in a presentation during the Production stage.

✓ **Left and Right.** One simple body language exercise that is excellent for beginners is the right and left hand signs. You can show them, that if you make an "L" with your thumb and index finger, your left hand will have a readable "L" which represents left. This is a fun exercise that will give them the ability to always know left and right when following or giving directions.

✓ **Word Errors.** You can also use body language to represent the error in a sentence by using your fingers accompanied with voice tone. For example, a lesson discussing past simple, the sentence "I go to the beach" is incorrect. Here you can use each finger to represent each word. I (thumb), go (index), to (middle), the (ring), beach (pinky). When pointing out the error, let your students correct themselves by saying the word "go" in a question tone while holding your index finger. They will catch on to this and some may even yell out the correct answer, "went!" Engage them to correct themselves, allow for those opportunities when the errors are minor and detailed explanation surrounding the error is not needed.

✓ **Reduce and Remix.** Sometimes your students will add parts to words for no reason at all and this is a good time to utilize a quick gesture as they speak, like the hand sign for cutting. You can also use this after the student is finished by saying the word in question again while using the hand sign for cut. Also, students can mix up words when speaking or reading and this is a good time to use body language to help guide your student to make a correction without actually interrupting verbally. A hand sign for remix is a fun way to implement some humor in corrections and your class and students will learn these signs and remember them for future lessons and corrections.

Other types of body language can help guide your students as they aim for accuracy and fluency in their exercises. They look to you, the teacher for ultimate approval and some simple body language can immediately alert them to their success or their mistakes in real time. Often times, in real English conversation we have specific non-verbal cues that let the people that are talking know that you are listening. A simple nod of yes lets your communication partner know you are following them, but on the other hand, a strange, confused or questioning look can give them a cue that something might not be understandable or correct. This is also true with smiling or lack of smiling, showing clear understanding or problems in communication. Your students can pick up on these non-verbal signs and they will understand immediately that something might not be correct in what they are doing. Using simple questioning voice tones can also help students pick up on mistakes, like "Hmmm?"

Creative Teacher Thinking

Why is using body language important to teaching? How would you use body language for tenses? How would you use body language for word errors in sentences? Can you think of some other great ways to use body language when teaching and making corrections?

Encourage Self-Correction

When teaching English as a foreign language, it is always important to remember that students make mistakes and learning a new language, often completely different than their native language is extremely difficult and sometimes frustrating. Put yourself in their shoes and imagine if you were beginning to learn their language, it can be a daunting thought in some cases and having that perspective can make you an exceptional teacher who nurtures students and gives them the ability to grow in their education and confidence. This being said, encouraging students to produce corrections on their own is an essential aspect to learning a new language in the long run.

You presented new material to your students in a clear and understandable way and in the Practice and Production stage, errors pop up here and there. This is your time to give your students the opportunity to make their own corrections, since they do know the material, but maybe just need a little help to get that correction on the tip of their tongue. There are a few ways you can approach self-correction with your students depending on the exercise and error.

First things first, give the non-verbal sign that something is incorrect and ensure the student has picked up on the mistake. If this non-verbal gesture brings no result, point out the specific area that needs to be adjusted to make the correction. After a small hint, you can move into a leading question that will allow your student to analyze the mistake and possibly warrant the correct answer. For pronunciation, repeating or echoing is essential for students to hear the correct way to say a word or phrase and will often stick with them as they strive for accuracy in the rest of their exercise.

✓ Give a non-verbal, body language cue pointing out the mistake.

- ✓ Use a small hint like tense, plural and so on to elicit the self-correction.
- ✓ Use leading questions that will allow your student to analyze the mistake deeper.
- ✓ Echoing is an important tactic for pronunciation mistakes.

Student to Student Corrections

There are a lot of benefits within student to student corrections. Remember that communication between students is important, even when it comes to corrections. The first thing you want to make sure is to have a good guideline set for corrections, that is, only positive and constructive corrections and feedback can be given in the classroom. A treat others as you would like to be treated atmosphere is always beneficial to have in place to ensure a positive environment where your students can feel comfortable and build confidence.

Student to student correction can allow you to see how deep the problem is within the class. If other students have problems correcting their classmates, you know that a more detailed review is in order to get the class back on track and moving in the right direction. Allowing peer correction can also help keep the atmosphere more relaxed as students can help their classmates by answering your leading questions if the student who made the error still can't find the correct answer. Student to student correction also ensures full class engagement as all students become a part of the correction process. Get your students involved and use the board, visuals, group echoing and other methods to keep your students on the right track when it comes to corrections.

Creative Teacher Thinking

What are the benefits of self-correction? What are some techniques you can use for self-correction? What are the benefits of student to student correction? Can you think of a great technique that can be useful for correction in student to student corrections?

Feedback Essentials

In your exceptionally well developed lesson plan, which outlines the Presentation, Practice and Production (PPP) as well as your Teacher Talk Time (TTT), should also contain some very important feedback time. Feedback time is essential for briefly reviewing the new material, going over corrections, answering questions and also giving out positive praise for completing the aim and objectives of the lesson. As an English language teacher, feedback time is important to give your students a sense of completion and overview of what to continue working on as well. Feedback time doesn't always need to be carried out at the end of a lesson and it is an adaptable feature of your lesson that you have control over depending on the material, exercise, class and so on.

Get creative with your feedback, just keep TTT low and allow your students to engage in the feedback time as a group. However, there are three main periods where you should think about conducting feedback time, of course depending on the lesson and other factors. Feedback after an exercise will get your students engaged as a group and will solidify the new material and is a good time to make corrections and get rid of any possible bad habits.

Another excellent time for feedback is of course, at the end of your lesson, discussing all things lesson oriented and engaging in questions about the new material. One period that most teachers find as a great time for feedback is at the end of the week. Going over the weekly lessons and reviewing each aim is an excellent way for you to review the week with your students and check how well they grasped and held onto the information.

Feedback is important and can be implemented in your lesson at various points, during the week, at the end of the week and so on. It gives your students and you that last chance to discuss new material and make sure everyone is moving in the right direction with a positive mindset, growing confidence and energetic enthusiasm.

Creative Teacher Thinking

Why is feedback important for you and your students? Think of a quick PPP outline for a lesson plan and write it down noting areas where feedback could be useful. What can you discuss in weekly feedback time with your students?

Writing Corrections

There will be times, depending on your student's level, where you will assign writing homework and thus having the important task of correcting it. Many of us can remember turning in our writing assignments and waiting for weeks to get it back and see the grade, not really giving much thought to the marks and slashes within the text. There is so much that goes into correcting writing, so many elements involved in the overall grade and guided feedback. Writing corrections are in many ways forms of non-verbal feedback represented by symbols, underlines and praise.

There are meanings behind the codes we use as teachers and many teachers use different abbreviations than others, but here are a few helpful ones to consider using. One note about codes used on writing assignments, make sure your students are familiar with your abbreviations so they can fully understand what exactly they need to correct or analyze as they reconstruct their paper if necessary.

- ✓ **?** = We use this when something is really not understandable and though it is vague, it will get the student thinking and can encourage communication with peers or with the teacher.
- ✓ **GR** = Grammar Mistake
- ✓ **SP** = Selling Mistake
- ✓ **WW** = Wrong Word
- ✓ **WT** = Wrong Tense
- ✓ **WO** = Wrong Order
- ✓ **Articles and Prepositions** = I normally circle them and let the student discover the the correct article or preposition to put in place of the mistake.

Some things to remember when using these abbreviations or any codes and/or abbreviations of your own are to make sure your students know what they mean and also check local meanings for these abbreviations and codes. Some things that we use in a common way may have negative meanings for another culture. Always stay culturally aware when teaching, it will keep you safe and employed.

Correcting within Structure

When analyzing your student's writing, it is important to look at the paper as a whole and within that whole are specific areas to review. The most important areas to cover are grammar, vocabulary, style, flow, and total exercise success. Check for grammar and vocabulary errors and mark mistakes with the appropriate codes. Look over the style and flow of the paper, is it formal or informal and does it link together well without strange transitions. A good flow of course is introduction, body (3 paragraphs or whatever's necessary) and conclusion. The most important of course is the paper's total success. Did your student cover the material you wanted covered and follow other guidelines that you would have shown when presenting the assignment.

Ensuring your students maintain a good structure, quality content without fillers or repetition and good use of tense throughout the paper is essential for correcting writing assignments. Give your notes and feedback and don't forget that positive feedback as well. Make sure to note the areas that are great and connected to the material by offering up some positive feedback in way of a "great point" or "well thought out!" This positive feedback will carry them into the next assignment with confidence and can also give them the energy to rewrite the paper in order to fix mistakes if you so choose. Some students learn from this as they fix their mistakes by rewriting the same paper, but keep in mind that some may feel it useless and giving them another assignment that could cover the same new material may be more appropriate.

Creative Teacher Thinking

What are some important things to do and consider when using codes and abbreviations when correcting writing assignments? What are the important areas to look over when correcting your students writing assignment (not just vocabulary)?

Testing

The testing process is important for your student's growth and there is an excellent way to discuss, administer, correct and have quality feedback time regarding testing. Having tests that cover the material covered after a few weeks or sections in a book is a great way to gauge progress and discover what needs your students still have when discussing the material they might not be completely comfortable with. A test can allow for positive and negative outcomes, depending on the student's success, but all situations surrounding testing can increase confidence, build knowledge, increase the positive atmosphere and trust as well as encourage communication.

There are many opportunities to conduct testing, allowing you to evaluate your student's competency. A good rule is weekly quiz with a test every three weeks if time allows for such a schedule. Reviewing information and letting your students show their stuff in testing is a great way to inhibit lifelong competency as opposed to monthly competency. Your testing outline should include a few very important elements that will encourage communication and set your students up for success and positivity.

1. **Presentation and Preparation:** Give your students the information they need, pop quizzes and unsuspected tests have shown to be ineffective for learning and causes unnecessary anxiety and negative feelings toward the content. Tell your students exactly when the test will be as well as outlining the key information they will need to study to be prepared.

2. **Feedback Session:** Allow for feedback about any issues they may have come across while reviewing for the test or quiz. This will allow them one last moment to clear up anything they might have misunderstood as well as keeping the entire class engaged in some pretest answers.

3. **Give the Test:** Administer the test in a positive way, whether it is an oral test or in paper form. Keeping positivity is a good way to encourage success and will start the process of turning any negative issues after the test into positive outcomes.

4. **Encourage Communication:** After the test is complete, let small groups grade their own tests using an answer key. This allows your students to understand what mistakes they made as they converse with their peers and discuss the test topics. Students can also use this time to do a bit of research together and search for the meanings behind the answers in their books and/or notes.

5. **Feedback Session:** The post-test feedback session is an important part of the whole testing process. What did we learn when our teachers gave us our test results at the end of class and sent us on our way? Usually nothing, and that is the method and environment you want to fight against. Let your students question the answers, ask for help on any issues and get the expert opinion, which is you the teacher. Feedback time after tests and quizzes are extremely important.

6. **100% Understanding:** After a test or quiz, ensure that everyone understands their mistakes and the corrections

100% and they feel confident and positive about the previous material and test. This is important and needs to be done before moving into the next lessons and compiling more information on new material.

Creative Teacher Thinking

Why is testing important? What are the key components to a positive and successful testing session and how often would you feel comfortable conducting testing and/or quizzes?

Chapter Nine

Utilizing Course Materials and Textbooks

Chapter Overview:

Material Outlook

The Published EFL/ESL Textbook

The Book and Student Balance

Grab Bag of Levels

Grab Bag of Ages

Text Material Structure

Creative with Lesson Material

Material Outlook

When you begin your teaching career as an English language teacher, you will find a variety of job choices that range from private one on one lessons, online classes, company classes, formal education schools and cram or tutor schools to name a few job options. With each new job position in any of the previously mentioned teaching atmospheres, comes a variety of teaching material and resources. However, in some cases, there might be no material and you will be on your own to develop a quality lesson surrounding material you produced or found online. Your creativity is essential and you will need to keep an organic approach as you give quality English language instruction while using the material available to you.

The Published TEFL Textbook

We have discussed the creation of exceptional lesson plans and we also know how important it is to get to know your students, their learning styles and of course their levels. You might find yourself excited to teach your first class of enthusiastic students and you will spend hours preparing fun and original material. This is great and your creativity and enthusiasm for teaching English will surely flow over to your student's enthusiasm to learn English, but time is always important to consider when putting together your lesson material. If you are spending hours and hours putting together the perfect material, than you will most likely burn out and begin to feel like you are not getting paid enough for all the time you are putting in. Understanding your work/life balance is very important in English language teaching. You might be in a beautiful new country, but spending all your time in your room developing endless material and not enjoying the very reason why you started teaching English as a foreign language in the first place, experience a new culture.

Some schools will have textbooks and other material for you to use, so don't be afraid to use it. Published EFL/ESL textbooks have many advantages and you can easily use them to create an excellent lesson plan with plenty of great material for all levels and learning styles. EFL/ESL textbooks provide your students and you with a great outline and structure as well as allowing you to track your student's progress as they work through the textbook exercises. There are in fact some disadvantages to textbooks and the biggest is the cost. If your students can gain access to the books, whether by purchasing them or having a classroom set available, this allows all of them to follow along as one. The problem with this is that textbooks are pricey and most English language teaching is done on a budget or in developing countries with no access or limited funds for the material and resources.

Published EFL/ESL textbooks often come in sets and they will cover all levels, from Beginner to Advanced levels with all the English language learning material you could hope for. There are also books that accompany these textbooks which offer great exercises and a follow along CD that will allow your students to hear conversations while following along in the text. There are so many English textbooks out there, listing them all would take a while. The best thing to do when thinking about what EFL/ESL textbooks to buy and use in your classes is research. Teacher forums, amazon reviews and cram school selections are a great way to decide which books are effective. To be honest, most of them follow a similar format and they all offer excellent content, it is how you use them and add them into your lessons that will make them effective for your students.

Creative Teacher Thinking

What are a few positive and negative aspects to using published EFL/ESL textbooks? Do you always have material available to you when teaching English as a foreign language? What is the most important thing to consider when you decide to use a specific EFL/ESL textbook?

The Book and Student Balance

Using an EFL/ESL textbook or another EFL/ESL type book is a great way to guide your lesson and have some support in material as you present new material to your students in the Presentation stage. Books are only as good as the way you use them in your lesson plan, so adapting the book material to fit your unique lesson is extremely important. There are many reasons to put your own spin on the lesson while still using a structured textbook. One is that, following a book structure in a section by section format can get quite boring and bring down class and student morale. Another reason is difference in level that is outside of your control, as well as a difference in age and interests, so it is important to develop a lesson using the textbook to meet each students needs and keep their interests peaked.

Grab Bag of Levels

Developing challenge that meets a student's level is important and you should always consider scale as well when using a textbook as lesson material. This being said, you may find yourself teaching to a class of multiple levels, that is, not everyone is the same level and some are a little ahead while others may be catching up to the middle of the pack. In English language teaching, this has become a common interference in the way we are able to develop our lesson plans and use material that fits and challenges all our students. This is where you can get creative and look deeper at the textbook material you would like to use for the majority of your students. Ask yourself, how can I adapt this material into a more challenging or less challenging exercise?

In order to know how you can adapt the text, think about your students and their levels. Chances are, they are not so far apart that you won't be able to find something challenging or less challenging for them to do. For students with a slighter higher level, you can give them some teacher tasks that will engage them in the material and at the same time challenge them. While the middle of the pack is reading or matching irregular verbs with their past simple verb forms, have your superstar students create sentences with the verbs, possibly even develop some kind of short story in a small paragraph or two. This gives them the challenge they thirst for and you can also use them as teachers, presenting what they have enveloped to the rest of the class. This exercise is also great with defining vocabulary in reading text as well as having them change a stories tense for further practice.

There are also great ways to keep your slightly behind students engaged and not frustrated by new material they can't quite understand yet. One tactic you can use for these students is to define the material and make side notes on the exercises. You can give your students these notes with a brief explanation to get them moving in the right direction. Within this one tactic, you can provide them with pictures of the book material to compliment the exercise and also change the format of an exercise to better fit the student's level. For example, an exercise that challenges the students to create a verb in a different tense may be too difficult, so you can change that exercise to a matching one instead, giving students choices and the ability to predict the answer by seeing a list of correct answers to choose from.

Another exceptional method for getting everyone up to speed is group and team exercises. This engages all students in communication and encourages them to support their peers that might not quite understand the new material. A team is only as strong as the weakest player, so you can use this as an advantage to keep the flow of communication thriving as they teach and help one another. Make sure you organize your groups appropriately, each group representing all levels of the class to ensure optimal learning and growth.

Creative Teacher Thinking

As an English language teacher, how can you develop a great lesson plan while using material from an EFL/EFL textbook? Some classes have multiple levels and there is no way to get around it, how would you develop a lesson based on an article that is focusing on past simple tense for students that are a little more advanced than the rest of the class? How can you use groups to develop a one level exercise?

Grab Bag of Ages

Age differences in a class is also another hazard of the English language teaching profession and is common among classroom settings set in companies or community based cram school courses.

Everyone's level is about the same, but the variety of age will dictate your lesson planning and the materials you choose to use in those particular classes. With age comes different interests, stages in life, family obligations, career variations, and sometimes, English learning goals. These are all things you will get to learn about while you get to know your students and you cannot please everyone with your choice in material. The best option in this scenario is to make your best effort at converting the textbook material into something each student can relate to. Remember, keeping lesson material relevant is extremely important and will keep your students engaged in the new material.

In order to develop a successful plan and convert your textbook exercise, look at the main points to what your aim and objectives will be. As long as those aims and objectives stay the same for each student, you can get creative and change the context of the textbook material to fit student interest. For example, a lesson on direction in the textbook will give the basic format of left, right, straight, north, south, and so on. Your students may live in the same city and you can use the textbook material as a warm-up before using an exaggerated tourist map of their city as material to keep them engaged. Ask questions like, "how do I get to your work from the square or another famous landmark?" This engages all students regardless of age and can make for exciting and fun communication between students and yourself.

Text Material Structure

Dealing with different levels and ages in your classroom can have obvious teaching obstacles, but you can overcome these barriers by keeping things relevant and building worth in your lesson structure. Textbooks are great and they offer ready-made material and an outline for you to follow, which is extremely useful for the creative teacher. Use textbook exercises and encourage your students to engage in side exercises that encompass the main objective of the textbook material. For example, an exercise covering the family tree can provoke excellent communication in a supplement exercise you developed in your lesson plan.

Here is an excellent outline for a family tree exercise based on textbook material:

1. **Warm-up activity:** Present vocabulary on family members by using visuals or even photos of your own family to peak your student's interest. Than have your students list everyone in their family in their notes or in the margins of a blank

family tree worksheet you prepared. Encourage questions and keep the warm up light and fun.

2. **Textbook activity:** Now is the time for your students to open there textbooks to the exercise covering family vocabulary and family tree (almost all English textbooks have this exercise). Since they already have some of the vocabulary from your presentation, this is their time to learn new vocabulary and learn how to piece together the family tree outline. Again, encourage questions before moving on.

3. **Supplement activity:** This is your student's time to put together their own family tree using what they know from your warm up exercise and the textbook exercise. Encourage group or table discussion as they piece it all together on the worksheet or in their notes. This is a great time for you to walk around the room and answer questions or make corrections. Once finished, they can than give short presentations to their partners or within their groups, maybe even to the whole class depending on how you develop the lesson plan.

4. **Cool down activity:** Here you can put their memories to the test by reshowing your family photos and ask them leading

questions about who is who and their relationships. Again, feedback and questions are always great to have here and will further more communication and class participation.

You can see the structure and lesson plan for important material using a textbook exercise with a little room for creativity. Another important note, don't let them see what is coming in the textbook before it is time. Looking at all of the new material at once can be overwhelming and may cause confusion before the new material is even presented. Have them focus on you and your Presentation before jumping into the textbook exercise.

Creative Teacher Thinking

How can you overcome age difference in the classroom? Can you think of any specific tactics to utilize? Structure is important in your lesson and even more so when implementing English textbook exercises. What are the key aspects to textbook material structure and what are the benefits of each?

Creative with Lesson Material

There is an endless sea of English language teaching material out there due to the need and high volume of people discovering English and the possible importance it may have on their life, whether for work, travel and/or for fun. The material you choose for your class can be the simplest of things, everyday items to online articles and English website exercises. The keys to using these materials are relevancy, specific message, visual context, connection with students and of course lesson time. We discussed connecting your students with new material using visual aids, photos, videos and/or slide shows and the importance of guiding your student's attention from the beginning of the lesson. Getting creative with your material is just that and it goes beyond the traditional forms of teaching.

When you get creative with your lesson material, you make the classroom atmosphere more exciting, fun and also allow for communication on new material in a positive way. An excellent example for an elementary class would be a basket of fruit or vegetables. This allows them to connect with real objects in a visual and tactile way that can encourage them to discover more about the new material in your amazing Presentation. Pass the fruit around, explain vocabulary, pronunciation and even encourage sentence development surrounding the new fruit or vegetables. You can even introduce a shopping scenario for higher level students and construct your very own produce stand in the classroom where students have to ask about prices and engage in common native speech.

Another great resource for material is the internet. There are several articles available from news sites and magazine websites that offer a wide variety of topics and information. The use of articles may be only appropriate for higher level students, but they have many advantages, including reading comprehension, vocabulary building, pronunciation practice, grammar use and the chance for your students to express their opinions and thoughts with a few guided questions from you the teacher.

There are also disadvantages to using online articles, whether it is news or popular magazine outlets. Some of these include preparation time, gauging the right article for your student's English level, the right length in regards to time and the general overwhelming presentation of information at one time. You have to decide what fits for your students and with a bit of creativity and exceptional planning, you can transform an article into a great lesson.

Here is a great example of using an online article in a lesson. This example article discusses bears as endangered species:

1. Ask your students what they know about the main subjects of the article (leading and open questions are good here).
2. Present 5 to 7 new vocabulary words, definition, antonyms, synonyms and a sample sentence or two.

3. Ensure all students are familiar with the new vocabulary and take a moment for questions.

4. Begin the article and allow your student to read out loud, alternating students between areas of the article. When they read out loud, you can note pronunciation errors and possible grammar issues. Between each section of reading, discuss these issues and make minor corrections.

5. Ask questions about the article material. Start with easy questions and work into more challenging ones.

6. Move into Practice/Production, remaining on the new material and focus. Sentences using new vocabulary or creating their own short article about bears.

Videos, movies and television shows are also great resources for developing material around your lesson plan. You can begin your lower level students with cartoons or videos with easy to understand vocabulary and grammar. Early English level students understand videos without a complicated storyline or plot better, so choose wisely as you move forward in your video selection. Remember, relevancy and level are very important. The last thing you want is half your class taking a nap during your video Presentation. Staying creative when developing your lessons is essential and no matter what you choose to use, it is your overall Presentation and connection with your students that counts.

Creative Teacher Thinking

What are some important factors to think about when using tactile material to help Present new information to your students? If you were given a spoon, bowl, cup and plate, what kind of lesson could you develop and how would you use that material?

Chapter Ten

Exceptional Classroom Management

Chapter Overview:

Manage with Ownership

Organize with Precision

Psychology of Organization

Setting Rules

Maintaining Control

Handling Issues

Manage with Ownership

In the workplace, there are managers and employees under that manager and in many ways, the classroom is no different. The manager gives direction, has more knowledge about the business and can ensure a sense of confidence and reliability in his team. Essentially, you are not just an English language teacher, you are a manager and your students are your team. If your management and leadership skills are not the best, your team will not be as strong and will hesitate to follow you. If your knowledge of the material is not vast, your team will not take you very seriously and their enthusiasm will be low. These are all things that you can relate to the classroom. You want your students to see you as a knowledgeable leader they can rely on and follow as they try to make sense of a new language, an already difficult task for them in some cases.

Classroom and student management is a very vast task that has many different moving parts to it and as a teacher, you must be aware of all those components. Where and when the class is to be held, lesson length, class size and level, classroom conditions, lesson plan, lesson material, flow of the actual lesson are just a few aspects to teaching. The important factor in all this is how you present yourself and conduct classroom etiquette while class is in session. You need to set boundaries that are clear for your students and you must follow these boundaries as well. Everyone liked the fun, easy going teacher, but there always needs to be an undertone of academic discipline and an action plan for the unruly students that may not be the best at staying within the boundaries you have set for the class.

Here are a few key points to keep in mind when managing your class:

- ✓ **Planning for Success:** We previously discussed planning for the unplanned and having a backup plan for when problems arise before and during your lesson. This may be an obvious piece of advice, but many teachers fail to have a plan of action in their lesson plans that will deal with or cover any problems. Take action and try to not be reactionary. Get as much information as possible and take into consideration anything that could happen.

✓ **Begin with Discipline:** It is always good to set the class tone from the very first lesson in the very first minute. This doesn't mean that you should be unfriendly, but set out the rules and guidelines for the class. Doing this will ensure that everyone is on the same page and adhering to the class rules will be one of the most important parts of the class. Give it to them straight and let it sink in before loosening up and moving into a more positive, fun atmosphere. Everyone should know that there are specific expectations between students and teachers, so it shouldn't come as a surprise when the rules are set.

✓ **Respect Gets Respect:** This should go without saying, respecting your students is extremely important. Do not make any assumptions about your students and treat them as you would like to be treated. This will keep a positive atmosphere in the classroom that encourages learning and builds confidence in your students. Also, do not let any students disrespect other students. It is important to maintain a classroom repeat level regardless who is involved.

✓ **Smile:** A smile is a great way to keep your students engaged and focused on you as you introduce all the new English material they will need to succeed. Let them enjoy learning and harbor a classroom of humor, fun and excitement, creating a lifelong experience of learning English. It's hard enough as it is, let your students enjoy it so they will continue learning.

✓ **Respect Time:** Respecting time is also an important attribute in teaching and it shows your students that you value their time and that you planned a lesson that is well developed and considerate. This is especially important when teaching to business professionals or career minded students.

Creative Teacher Thinking

Why is classroom management important and what does it involve? What are three key points to managing your classroom and why would these be important to you?

Organize with Precision

The organization process is an entirely organic project. You can use your creativity, depending on the exercise you are doing, what is in your lesson plan and what works best for your students. There are also outside factors in many cases, like not enough chairs, limited table space and sometimes a lack of all things in general, no board, chairs and/or tables. Harness your creativity and stay calm as you piece together an excellent, welcoming classroom for your enthusiastic students.

Here are a few areas to consider when thinking about organizing your class with precision:

✓ Always find out the number of students so you can begin planning a strategy before you show up.

✓ Where is the classroom, is it in a loft above machine equipment that will be running during your class? You need to try as hard as you can to create a quiet atmosphere that nurtures learning.

✓ How big is the room and is it a traditional style set up or is the room a weird shape, maybe an old office converted into a learning or break room area? Knowing the layout will also help you be an effective classroom planner.

✓ Is it bright enough for you and your students to see? A dark classroom means a sleepy class, so this is an important aspect to consider. Also, make sure there is enough light on the board so students can easily see the information without getting a migraine from squinting for an hour.

✓ Is there a solid infrastructure in the classroom? Is their internet access and electrical outlets available for you to plug in a projector or computer? Important depending on how you develop your lesson plan and which material or aids you will use for the class instruction.

✓ Is there enough furniture to fit the class and can you move it to create the atmosphere you want? I have been in many classrooms with not enough chairs and you will most likely run into this too. Don't waste your student's time by taking class time to find chairs or tables. Know how many students you will have and get the room ready beforehand.

✓ Last but not least, keep the temperature comfortable. It can be frustrating to freeze or sweat to death while trying to understand a foreign language. Get to class early and make the room welcoming and at a comfortable temperature for when your students arrive.

Of course, some of these things can't be avoided and you have to get creative and think on your feet. You might be teaching at an international factory or in a small village in a developing country. Do the best you can with what you got and going the extra mile when you can, will make you a great teacher in the eyes of your students. If you can, personalize your classroom and encourage your students to do so as well. This increases the comfort level and allows for a better learning environment.

Psychology of Organization

There are a few ways to physically organize your classroom to encourage learning and optimize communication. The horseshoe layout is an excellent way to get your students relaxed in an orderly manner. The students can see one another, you, the board or any other key visual you may want to present. It also allows for a stage like space in the middle for Production or Practice exercises. The next layout focuses on small groups and is great for pre organizing your students into groups or pairs while encouraging communication when it is appropriate. It is a good idea to stagger the rows in order to avoid a linear block system the traditional layout has.

In groups, your students can communicate with one another; see you and the board with only a little adjustment on their part. There is always the traditional layout, one desk after the other in linear rows. This is great for traditional teaching, but in English language teaching, you want to establish a more open and communicable environment. Again, get creative to optimize learning and communication while maintaining control.

Creative Teacher Thinking

What are a few aspects to consider when organizing your classroom? If you had a class of 7 students with enough chairs and tables, how would you organize your classroom to enhance learning?

Setting Rules

Setting the class rules are important to do the first day in the first minute or within reason, maybe introduce yourself briefly and cover the rules and then move into further introduction and getting to know your students. Rules are important for various reasons, but mainly, you want to create a safe, positive environment where students can feel free to ask questions, make mistakes and build confidence as fast as they learn English. That is the main goal when it comes to classroom rules and most students have participated in a classroom structure before, so some rules should be very familiar.

Here are a few rules to keep in mind and of course you can add to this list when you take on your very own class:

- √ **Be on Time:** Attention to detail is important when learning English and attention to time should be also put on the important list for your students. Students should arrive on time, so class can start when it is scheduled. When students are late, it slows down the flow of the class and it may affect other students negatively.

- √ **Cell Phones Off:** In today's classroom, the cell phone, personal computer, tablet, kindle and any other device can be a distraction to your class. It is important to remind your students that complete focus for the entire duration of the class is important. Make sure they realize that in order to be respectful, they should turn off their phones or any other personal electronic device and store them out of site.

- √ **Respect:** Setting up a classroom environment that is centered on respect will ultimately encourage positivity and a willing to learn in your students. Students should respect you, the teacher, as well as all the other students in the class. No bad words, bullying, make fun of another student, and/or general disruption of the class. Remind them that disrespect of any kind will get them eliminated from the class with lithe hesitation.

✓ **Be Prepared:** Students should be prepared for class when they arrive on time, ready to learn. They expect you to be on time and ready to teach and have the proper material needed for them to learn, so make sure they know to also bring the appropriate material needed for success (paper, books, writing utensils, dictionary and great attitude).

✓ **Food and Drinks:** The traditional rule of no food or drinks is a debatable one and in some respects, having water or a non-alcoholic beverage can help the student stay comfortable. Food, however, is a different subject and it will be up to you to set this rule. It may depend on factors of age in some instances, but it is a teacher judgment call.

Creative Teacher Thinking

When should you set classroom rules? Why is it important to set up rules in your classroom, why not just let things happen, after all, most students should know the general rules anyway?

Maintaining Control

With the rules delivered clearly, double check and make sure that everyone in the class flu understands them and they have no problems with following them. The first step to maintaining control of your students is to make sure the rules are clear and concise with every student onboard with them. You want your students to feel comfortable in class and willing to put themselves out there a little in order to learn effectively. You also want your students to build confidence and be able to speak English without hesitation or worry of sounding dumb. Maintaining control allows everyone to stay focused on the main topic, learning English effectively during the entire length of the lesson.

Here are some essential aspects to keep in mind when thinking of how to maintain control of your students each lesson, creating a consistent positive learning environment:

1. **Class Language:** Teaching some basic classroom language is extremely important for your students. It will allow them to ask questions, correctly address the class or teacher and keep their language focused on English.

Some great examples of classroom language are:

✓ Can you please repeat the question?

✓ I don't understand.

✓ I understand.

✓ Can you write that on the board please?

✓ What page in the book.

✓ What does that mean?

✓ Can you explain more?

✓ Common words that are important for the class (section, paragraph, word, sentence, read, write, listen, speak or say and so on).

2. **TR - ST Talk Time:** Establishing clear rules regarding when students can speak with one another is also important to keep

in mind when maintaining control. They should understand that when you begin speaking, all student conversation should stop and they should turn their devoted attention toward you and only you. This is especially important during the Presentation stage when introducing the material is crucial to the rest of the lesson.

3. **Yellow Card and Red Card:** Most students around the world that are learning English as a foreign language have knowledge of "soccer" or "football." This can be a great way to establish a consistent penalty system when dealing with students that wish to disrupt the class or break the rules. Remember, there is really no need to get into any verbal discussion and soccer is a good example of establishing someone committed a penalty and they receive a warning, which will result in disciplinary action if continued. This system sets a clear warning and discipline ratio.

4. **Consistent and Fair:** No one likes a referee who is inconstant with giving out penalties. Stay consistent in your yellow cards and red cards, sticking to the rules set by you will ensure that students retain respect for your rules regardless of who is breaking them. This parallels fairness,, something that is important to keep trust and positivity in

your classroom. Playing favorites will result in mutiny and the learning environment will collapse.

5. **Take Care of Business:** Do not let a situation go further than it has to. Politely deal with the student and move the focus back to the lesson. Don't let the rest of the class suffer, because of one student's actions. Inform the student of his/her infraction and give the required punishment and then continue with teaching. If you are teaching in a school or teaching company classes, utilize upper management to help you deal with any reoccurring issues.

Creative Teacher Thinking

What are two ways of maintaining control of your students that are important to you? How would you deal with a student who first says a bad word, then laughs at another student's question and thus continues to be disruptive by speaking in his native language? Describe how you would deal with each infraction of your rules.

Handling Issues

Depending on the size of the class, student background, age and so on, problem students may arise and will test you and other students will watch and take note of how you deal with the problem.

Generally, students do not act out unless there is an underlying problem that needs to be addressed. Don't just write the student off as a bad student who doesn't want r care to learn English. Most problem students are either bored with the material, because they are ahead of the class, a different level. Or the problem student is behind the class and doesn't understand the material or what's going on, thus they shut down and act out. These students can be turned around and put into the right direction if you pay close attention to what is really going on with the student.

Here are a few problems that may arise during your class and a few tips on how to resolve the situation:

1. **The Bully:** In some extreme cases, you might find yourself in the midst of a class bully and this problem is an issue that destroys the positive and confident atmosphere you have worked hard to develop in your classroom. In the case of bullying, dispatch the student immediately from the class and take an immediate red card stance as punishment. You may be the first teacher or even person to take a harsh stand against the student's behavior and this will cause him to self-reflect and think about his actions. This is also a god time to share why bullying is inappropriate and take some time with the problem student after class to see what is going on, why

he or she is acting out this way. Showing concern will win trust and it could encourage positive change.

2. **The Smart Attention Seekers:** There are some students that are indeed more advanced than the rest of the class and if you can't move them up a level or if you just noticed their level separation, you will be forced to deal with them. Remember, they are showing off and asking questions and giving answers, because they are most likely bored with the material. They are acting out and most likely, waiting for you to challenge them. During class, move on to other students for answers and questions, keep the whole class involved and don't let the student take control. After class, set the challenge to the student and ask him to prepare a report or essay, maybe even have them develop a Presentation on some new material they think is important. You can have this student present it to you or the class depending on the validity of the material and this is also a good time for you to make sure he is definitely at a higher level than the class.

3. **Subject Changers:** When students become bored or restless, they may want to change the subject or focus of the class by asking questions with no to little relevancy of the material you are presenting to the class. Keep these students at bay

and maintain control of the class by keeping all eyes and ears on you and not the student acting out. Remind him or her that when you are speaking, students listen. After class, address the issue with the student and let him or her speak or ask the questions that were so important to ask during the lesson. You can keep this situation positive and again, find out the real issue. Maybe the student is at a different level and need more or less of a challenge to stay focused during the lesson.

4. **Communication Breakdown:** There may be times when you present to the class and begin to encourage discussion and communication, but there is only silence and lost eyes staring at you. This could be many things, but most likely, it is your general enthusiasm while teaching or they don't understand the material or exercise clearly, which means your Presentation needs adjustment. Start with your attitude, check yourself and make sure you are smiling and enthusiastic. You can even switch gears and get the students engaged in some off topic stuff, just to break the ice and get the discussion flowing again. Next could be the material and you may have to implement an exercise that is easier or an activity will bring groups together in discussion. Get creative in these situations, communication is the most important factor when

learning English and it must exist in the lesson for it to be an effective class.

Creative Teacher Thinking

What are some key points to dealing with problems? How do you deal with a bully in your classroom? Are all problem students just bad and there is nothing you can do? Explain why or why not?

Chapter Eleven

Teaching Reading Essentials

Chapter Overview:

Is Reading Important?

The Reading Material

What's the Word?

Sentence Structure and Reading

Reading Time and Length

Is Reading Important?

Reading is the cornerstone to learning a language and it is extremely important to implement into your syllabus. Reading compliments all the other important aspects of the English language, listening, speaking and of course writing. Reading can reveal new words, point out pronunciation errors, raise questions about the material being read, promote self and thought expression, create positive reading comprehension and shows how the language is structured grammatically. There is so much involved with reading and your students can benefit from reading lessons and also encourage them to begin reading English articles, books and/or short blogs which often contain native speech phrases and more common English language.

The Reading Material

When deciding what material to use in your reading lessons, it is good to consider a few things when browsing the internet or library for class resources. The internet is a great source for reading material with all the news articles, popular magazine material, blogs, excerpts from books and so on. Choose wisely, because if your reading material is too difficult or too easy, students can become frustrated and/or bored and cause for a dislike in reading that will carry on, lesson after lesson, dreading each reading exercise.

When choosing your reading material, consider these aspects:

✓ What is the level of your students? Think about what they should know at this level (see chapter one) and consider what you have introduced to them in the previous lessons. The material should fit their level with room for vocabulary building and pronunciation practice.

✓ Keeping things relevant has become a reoccurring theme and you should consider relevancy and also goals within the student's reasons for learning English. Maybe your student is a business professional and wants to expand vocabulary for work. Finding articles on business will go a lot further than say, articles on home and gardening. Relevancy is key!

✓ Age is also a factor when choosing your reading materials. Age can dictate interest and it is also important to make sure the reading material is appropriate for your student's age group. I found that most young students know the same childhood stories as English natives and when they read the story in English, it is easier since they already have a good idea of the plot and storyline.

✓ Finding the right balance of challenge is important when choosing your reading material as well. Too easy will cause boredom and too much will cause frustration. Find a good balance and don't feel that you have to stick to the material. Feel free to expand on the main topic as it relates to your lesson aim, asking questions that will encourage communication and check competency at the same time are good tactics in reading exercises.

✓ Time length is also an important factor to consider. Depending on the article length, you might find that time runs out before the article and material is fully read and discussed. This can also go the other way, finishing too early, which is not as much of a problem, but be ready with supplemental activities for your students to further their understanding of the material.

Creative Teacher Thinking

We discussed structure of using articles as learning material in Chapter 5. and in this chapter we covered considerations when choosing reading material for your lesson. Give a brief outline of a lesson that uses reading material for a student who is 15 years old, female and has an intermediate level. Also, what is important to consider in this lesson?

What's the Word?

Most of us learned words in school by reading, seeing the word, reading the definition of the word, seeing how the word is used in a sentence, making our own sentences using the word and then the dreaded vocabulary test every Friday covering all the new words of the week. Most of how we learn a new word is associated with reading and seeing how that word is ultimately used within a general context. This is why reading is so important for English learners and you are essentially doing the same as you were once taught.

Before presenting the reading material, you should have some preset vocabulary to introduce to your students that will be discovered in the reading material. Write these on the boarder have them somewhere your students can reference them during the reading. During the reading, students will naturally discover other words as they read and it is important that you write these words somewhere as a reference and to discuss the new words afterwards. The same goes for pronunciation words, put them on the board after using and echoing the correct pronunciation. Chances are, if your students can't pronounce a word, they most likely won't know the meaning as well.

Here are a few essential pronunciation tips for you to introduce to your students before any reading lesson:

✓ Words that begin with **Wh**, like **wh**en, the **h** is silent and only the **w** is pronounced.

✓ Words that begin with **Wr**, like **wr**ite, the **w** is silent and only the **r** is pronounced.

✓ Words with the letter **s** between to vowels, like pre**s**ent, changes to a **z** pronunciation.

✓ Words with **Th**, like **th**at, are pronounced with a **tha** sound. The tongue goes to the front of the mouth and rests under the top front teeth.

✓ Words with a consonant in front of a **n**, like **kn**ife or **gn**arly, only the **n** is pronounced.

These are a few of the most common issues students struggle with and are important to cover. Some students from different regions of the world have their own pronunciation issues, like Asian countries and Japan, their use of words with r and l are often mispronounced. Be aware of the cultural issues regarding English pronunciation and plan for these issues. Taking time to quell specific pronunciation problems before reading exercises can be beneficial to you and your students.

Creative Teacher Thinking

What are a few methods you can use to help your students understand new words during reading lessons? Would it be beneficial to address common pronunciation mistakes before a reading lesson? Why or why not?

Sentence Structure within Reading

When it comes to English language learning with the use of reading material in a reading lesson, this is reading and then there is reading correctly. Students often sound like robots from another planet when reading and sometimes it has to do with their confidence and other times it is punctuation and understanding the structure of a sentence. To get your students reading more confidently and with better flow and tone, let's look at the components of a sentence first. There are many aspects to a sentence and these aspects will dictate how your students read. For example, a sentence with a question mark can change how it is read.

For example: "Did she really say that?" or "Really?" creates a tone in the voice of the reader to illustrate the question. This is one scenario where a simple **(?) question mark** can change meaning, tone and sentence structure.

Here are some punctuation marks that can dictate how a sentence is read:

✓ **Period Mark:** The **(.)** shows that a sentence has come to a complete end and the student should pause here before continuing to the next sentence. Also explain how the period is used in abbreviations before they discover this in a sentence and it causes confusion.

✓ **Quotation Marks:** Quotation marks **("")** are used to show what a person has actually said.

- ✓ **Apostrophe:** Using an apostrophe (') notifies the reader that something is possessive or there is an abbreviation.
- ✓ **Colon:** The colon (:) is used in lists, noting an example, and/or giving more detail about something mentioned previously.
- ✓ **Comma:** Using a comma (,) is essential for a reader to know that there is a pause or separation from one sentence or word to the next.
- ✓ **Hyphen:** A hyphen (-) is used when you want to combine two words.

There are so many different types of punctuation marks and this is just a short list of a few important ones. As a teacher of English, familiarize yourself with the many different punctuation marks out there in the English language. These are essential for your students to understand structure in reading sentences within a body of text. When your students have a great understanding of this material, it can be applied to writing as well. We will discuss writing lessons in the next chapter, Chapter Twelve.

It is also very important that you practice what you preach and make sure that you are not lazy in your own writing when it comes time for your students to read it. Remember, your students are always watching you and they will begin mimicking your speech and writing habits. This is true not only for young learners, but also adult and career minded students. Another important note on reading is to make sure you let your students develop a reading voice, so they don't all sound like English reading robots. It is sometimes helpful to refer to a celebrity voice or possibly even show them how to read in a more musical way. This allows them to gain more confidence and transition from one sentence to the next easier.

Creative Teacher Thinking

What are some helpful ways to show your students the different punctuation marks and how they should be noted while reading a sentence or body of text? What would be a good strategy for letting your students develop a great reading voice with natural flow and transition, not the English robot?

Reading Time and Length

Reading time and length is an important aspect to teaching reading and it is often overlooked when teaching a reading class. Some teachers take the approach of one student reading one page and the next reading the next page and so on. This is a good lesson plan, but often times more useful after students develop the necessary skills and have a full understanding of sentence structure and punctuation marks.

First things first, get the basics out of the way. Let them commit the punctuation marks to memory as they piece together sentences that you have provided, filled with punctuation and transition. Make it fun after that, read like a robot and let them hear and feel how uninteresting it is to listen to that style of reading. You can then give some great examples of clear, educated reading voices, think famous actors narrating films (a popular penguin movie)! This will give them the "what not to do first" and then the, "wow, I want to sound like that motivation after." It is essential for your students to develop a clear voice while pausing and changing their tone throughout as the sentence changes with punctuation.

After you establish these key factors, move them into more lengthy paragraphs, maybe two to three sentences and go from there. You want to make sure that they are not reading more than three minutes at a time. Remember, you want them not just reading, but also understanding what they are reading at the same time. When beginning, anything over three minutes may begin to become blurry and the first part of the paragraph may have been lost to new parts in the end. You can adjust with your student's growth, but keep an eye on length and time. Keeping it short will keep a more creative and fun atmosphere in the beginning. Build their confidence and they will blossom quickly.

Chapter Twelve

Getting into the Reading Lesson

Chapter Overview:

Keep It Fun, Keep It Relevant

Ready, Set, Read

Warm Ups

Reading Comprehension

New Vocabulary

Reading Lesson Checklist

Keep It Fun, Keep It Relevant

When your students begin to catch on and their reading has great flow, transition, and they are hitting all the proper pauses and so on, you will need to find interesting material. It is fine at first to have some basic material with little relevancy, but as their reading comprehension grows, they will want reading material that interests them. This all comes down to knowing your students and their levels. Utilize reading material that includes some English concepts that have been previously discussed. For example, a story about a ranch or farm will compliment animal and outdoor work vocabulary very well. Engage them from all sides with your relevancy and they will maintain enthusiasm for reading.

Creative Teacher Thinking

What are some key aspects behind reading time and length? Why is it important to consider relevancy when choosing your reading material? Explain your strategy for teaching a few reading sentences to an elementary student interested in running marathons.

Ready, Set, Read

Before you begin your reading lesson, you have a few things to consider. Why are my students reading this? What are some questions I can ask about the reading material? How will I address vocabulary and pronunciation issues? What will be my Production exercise that will complement the reading? These are all great questions to ask yourself before jumping into a reading lesson and as we discussed before, planning is the key to a successful lesson where aims and objectives are met.

Warm Ups

Think of learning like exercise. You need to stretch and get ready before a run, get nice and loose before the main activity. This also goes for teaching English as a foreign language, and teaching anything. Before having your students hop into well thought out reading material, think about a fun exercise you can implement to get the warmed up and thinking about the overall topic in English. This can be achieved in a few different ways and it can not only be fun, but create an enthusiastic student before he or she even sees the reading material. For example, let's say you want your students to read a small article on bears and why they hibernate. You can first by showing a picture of a bear, maybe even a video. After that, you can begin asking questions about a bear's life, what it eats, what it might do in the summer and then the main topic of the article, what the bears do in the winter, hibernate.

In your reading exercise warm up, you can also find a few vocabulary words that are associated with the main topic and in the text of the article. Our example of bears and hibernation, you can give five to seven vocabulary words relating to the article, like hibernation and any other word you feel might be new to your students. They will of course find other new words, but introducing a few before they find them in the article will boost their confidence and also serve as a great warm up exercise. You can also engage your students with questions that will get their imagination running in the right direction. Remember relevancy and keep the warm up fun and creative.

Reading Comprehension

After your students are all stretched out and warmed up, let them see the course they are about to run by handing out the material or having them turn to the page in their books, giving them a few moments to look it over. This is not a totally necessary aspect, but it does further the student's engagement of the reading material and you can even ask a few questions about what they think they are about to read. This should be short, not spending a great amount of time on this; however, it is a useful tool to consider.

Ask your students open questions about what they think the text is about and what they expect to find while reading. You could even develop a few short multiple choice questions or even read a part of the introduction to get it started and have a few follow up questions ready for your students. Peak their interest from the get go and enthusiastic reading in the exercise will follow. They will want to see if their prediction of the main topic is correct while developing creative ideas about the main subject and characters.

Another important aspect of reading lessons are the follow up or comprehension questions you will ask them as you all work through the material together. Engage them on the subjects and important aspects they have just read. You can do this by individual or make it a group effort. If your students just read a section discussing the food a bear consumes before hibernation, ask them to summarize that section or have them tell you how much food the bear consumes or what type of food. This will allow your students to build confidence and work through the material with a clear understanding as well as give you a good idea of how they comprehend what they are reading.

You can also have them predict what is going to happen in the story next. We all enjoy a good television series that intrigues us and we often discuss it with our friends and family. Make them predict the next part of the story by using what they already know and this will engage them further into the material and also give value to what they are reading. Follow up questions and open ended summarizations of the reading material is very useful at the end and will give you a great idea of who fully understands while having your students explain it to their peers. The ending summary by your students can be a good practice or even production exercise. Think book club or movie review!

Creative Teacher Thinking

What are some helpful questions you should ask yourself when developing your reading exercise lesson plan? What is the value of warm ups? Outline a quick lesson plan regarding a reading lesson from warm up to an ending summary.

New Vocabulary

When discussing vocabulary, it is important to remember what is relevant and what we use in native English communication on a regular basis. Most of your students will be focusing on daily communication and not taking a graduate school exam, so the big words no one uses can be discarded until a later date. Keeping the vocabulary relevant to your student's goals and level is just as important as keeping the material relevant. As we discussed in the warm up stage, you can outline a few words that will be found in the text that you think may be relevant to their learning growth. It is also inevitable that your students will find some words in your reading material that will be knew. Any word they cannot pronounce, you can definitely note as a possible new word.

When new words are naturally discovered in the reading material, it is better to let the student move on with his or her reading as they make a note of the word by underlining it. One effective method is for you the teacher to note any mispronounced words while encouraging your students to underline or remember the words that might not be so familiar. When they have completed their reading section, you can than share your mispronounced words first and then ask them what words are new to them. This strategy will open the lines of communication and help them feel more comfortable asking questions. Most of the time, you will have picked out the words they want to ask about anyways. Keep their confidence high and encourage a free to ask any question classroom as long as it is focused on the main topic.

You can also encourage your students to look up their words if dictionaries are available and share what they find with the class. This is a great way to develop group cohesion and it will also save some lesson time. One strategy that is useful is to ask the students what they think a word means before giving them the definition. Sometimes the word is a variation of a word they may already know. A prefix or suffix can play tricks on your students when it comes to vocabulary, so let them give it a try first. Most importantly, keep the definitions and explanations in English. Associating a word with their native language is helpful, but it is not a long term learning concept. Approach all new English words in English!

Reading Lesson Checklist

1. Ask yourself the essential reading exercise questions while developing your amazing lesson plan.
2. Develop some visual aids and keep in mind how many students you have and how many reading materials you need.

3. Warm your students up before giving them the reading material to look over. Engage them on the topic of the reading material before they even know what it is about! Here you could even introduce helpful and relevant vocabulary.

4. Let them see, look over, and begin making assumptions about what they will read. Ask them some questions about what they think the article or story will be about after they have a short period of time to look it over.

5. Reading with mindfulness to length and time. Follow up each student or section with follow up questions to check reading comprehension and allow for predictions.

6. Overall summary and questions about what your students have read and what they think about it. Maybe a Production activity would be useful here!

7. Feedback!

Creative Teacher Thinking

What are a few strategies for dealing with new vocabulary? Develop a quick lesson plan using reading material of your choice. Follow the reading lesson checklist and make sure to account for time of each part in your lesson plan.

Chapter Thirteen
Writing Lesson Essentials

Chapter Overview:

Why and When?

Filling the Blank Page

Developing Sentence Structure

The Paragraph

Lesson Format

Warm Ups

Warm Up Discussion

Warm Up Outline

Timing Student Writing

Why and When?

In many instances, you will have students that want to take their communication skills to the next level and begin writing in a different language. If they are reading well and have a good understanding of sentence structure, page outline, subject outline, and punctuation, writing can be a somewhat painless transition. It will take time for your students to begin writing academic style papers with cohesive subject matter, but we all had to start somewhere. You can guide your students from sentence to paragraph, to a whole body of work with patience and exceptional lesson planning. It is always a great idea to incorporate a little writing in your classes since many students will eventually have to write something in English at some point. Instances include when on vacation, emails to foreign friends and native English speaking colleagues.

Filling the Blank Page

When approaching writing, you should ensure that your students are ready. This is not something a basic level student should be working on since they have yet to read consistently and fully comprehend the structure of sentences in any real form. Again, make sure it is level appropriate, otherwise your student may become frustrated and take a disliking to the lesson and writing all together. Another important thing to remember when teaching your students writing, is to make sure that they are understanding the material and understanding each exercise or example before moving on to the next. You want to eliminate bad habits in writing before they develop!

If you have students with the ability to formulate sentences in writing, you are a step ahead of the curve, but often times, you may have to begin from the basics and develop their skills overtime. A good way for your students to begin developing basic writing skills is to encourage them to copy any and everything you write on the board. You can also have them take notes and write their thoughts and new vocabulary words in their notebooks. This will get them moving in the right direction and peek in from time to time and make sure what they are writing is bad habit free and it is working in their favor. You can even have them write small sentences from the get go of each class to get them engaged in writing. A little at a time goes a long way in learning English.

Developing Sentence Structure

Good sentence structure comes down to one thing, a good understanding of grammar. It is essential for your students to know how to join nouns and verbs, place subjects and adjectives in the right place, and have cohesion in their sentence. Many English learners will have some habits that are from their own native languages and it is important to recognize if they are applying their own grammar rules to their English writing. Having your students write good, grammatical sentences as they learn grammar in the early levels is the key to success down the road. For example, if your student is learning how to describe something during a grammar lesson discussing adjectives, have them write it down or copy your board work.

✓ **His red hat.** This is an example and something you may hear or see. Correct these bad habits as soon as you find them.

✓ **His hat is red. Or, he has a red hat.** This would be something they would communicate verbally and write as well.

Implementing writing in production exercises can also be an effective way for your students to start putting what they learn in grammar lessons to use with writing. It is also important to cover prepositions and describe how they are used to connect words in a well-developed sentence. You could have your students write a few sentences covering material on irregular verbs used in short sentences. You could also have them use new adjectives to describe their surroundings in the classroom. These are all great ways to get your students thinking English when writing. It is also important to double check your higher level students and make sure they are in fact writing in a proper way. Many of them may have picked up quite a few bad habits over the years and it is good to clarify what they should be doing correctly before letting them loose on a longer body of writing.

Creative Teacher Thinking

How can you encourage your early English level students to write? What is something to focus on when looking at your student's writing? How can bad habits have a long term affect?

The Paragraph

The transition into developing paragraphs can begin after your students show a solid comprehension of sentence structure and are developing good, grammatically sound sentences. The transition may be a bit harder than you might expect, since there are new rules surrounding paragraph development. You will have to develop one lesson to convey the outline of a good paragraph and how each paragraph will address a different area or aspect of the main idea, but still maintaining a good flow in the paragraph transition. The best way to show your students how to develop their paragraphs is by using a beginning topic sentence that moves into supporting sentences. Remember, presentation is key to a good practice. Develop some excellent visual aids and examples to make sure they fully understand how to construct a great working paragraph.

Here is an example of a basic outline for paragraph structure:

1. **Topic Sentence.** This sentence will be the main explanation to what the paragraph will be about.

2. **Supporting Sentence.** A sentence that supports the topic sentence by using facts, ideas, theories, and/or opinions.

3. **Supporting Sentence.**

4. **Supporting Sentence.**

This outline can be used to show the students a good structure before they start writing what we would recognize as a paragraph. For the topic sentence, ask them what they will be writing their paragraph about. Have them put a well-structured sentence on their topic in number one. You will have them continue this outline by placing supporting sentences in the following areas two through four or however many supporting sentences they have. It is good to present them with an outline of your own and ensure they are following the structure.

After they have outlined their topic sentence and supporting sentences, you can move into connecting one through five (or however many they have) using linking or connecting words. Linking or connecting words are the glue that sticks are sentences together and gives them smith transition from one sentence to the next. We use them without thinking, but for an English learner, they can often be overwhelming since they are often paired with a form of punctuation. So, but, and, because, before, and however are all great connecting words that you can teach your students in order for them to develop their very own paragraphs.

Once they have a fluid understanding of the connecting words, you can let them loose to create their paragraph using their outlines as a guide and connecting or linking words to glue it all together. It is important to mention to your students that connecting words are not always used and overusing them can interrupt or shadow their writing message. A good way to describe the use of connecting words and developing their paragraphs is to once again, offer exceptional examples and build their confidence with open communication on the subject. You can even spark some group creativity as each member of the group develops one part of the paragraph based on the sentence before theirs. Get and stay creative with your students, watch for bad habits, and your student's writing will grow.

Creative Teacher Thinking

How would you approach teaching your students to write paragraphs? What is important to make sure of before transitioning to a lesson on writing and constructing paragraphs? Are connecting and linking words necessary? Can connecting or linking words be overused?

Writing Lesson Format

Your writing lesson format will be similar to your reading lesson, only your students will be writing and it may be a little more difficult for you to check-in with your student's comprehension as often as in reading. Your mobility will be important as you float around the room and watch them craft their paragraphs. There are however, some questions you need to ask yourself when developing your writing exercise lesson plan. Just as in the reading lessons, these key points are very important for student and teacher success in meeting the lesson's aims and objectives.

Here are some key aspects to consider when developing your writing lesson plan:

✓ Is my material relevant? This is important in everything we present to our students and keeping your material interesting and at the appropriate English level will keep your students engaged in the material and happy to learn more.

✓ Who is the student's audience? Giving your students a clear picture of who they will be writing for or to will allow them to construct qualitative writing. This will also be important when discussing the topic of formal and informal writing styles.

✓ Do my students have a good understanding of the writing exercise or task? This is of course very important and should be considered when developing your material and also presenting it to your students. Using examples and visual references can guide your students to success in their writing assignments.

These are three key points when taking a deeper look into the writing lesson you want to develop for your students. Giving them the tools to succeed are important and it will encourage them to fulfill their writing goals as they build confidence in an often overwhelming task. Writing may be scary for some students since they are on their own to create a piece of work, essentially with little interaction from you and their classmates. This is also why class engagement is important before the writing task begins.

Creative Teacher Thinking

What are our three writing lesson aspects and why is each one important when developing your writing lesson plan? What is an important task to complete before the writing task begins?

Warm Ups

Just as we discussed in Chapter Twelve, Reading development and Instruction, warm ups are an intricate part of the lesson. Warm ups develop classroom communication and allow your students to communicate and brainstorm with you, the teacher, and their classmates in group or pair discussion regarding the writing topic. This is a great aspect of writing lessons, since they will have little communication during the actually exercise, which requires them to think, be creative, and write on their own.

Warm Up Discussion

Develop class discussion around the chosen writing topic. This method will not only introduce the main topic your students will write about, it will allow them to begin the creative process while learning about the topic at the same time. If you want your students to write about a specific place, you would introduce that place to them by using a visual aid to help guide the discussion in the right direction. For example, a writing topic on the Golden Gate Bridge in San Francisco, California can begin with a photo or short video of the bridge itself. Engage them with visual stimulation and then follow up with some essential discussion questions that will help them write creatively and effectively.

Here is a brief outline of a warm-up discussion using a visual aid:

1. Show your students a photo or video of the Golden Gate Bridge. Let them see the photo or pause the video at a specific place so they can use that as a visual reference.
2. Give students the basic information they may need regarding the bridge's detailed information by using questions before giving them the correct information. An example would be, "when was the Golden Gate Bridge built?" Allow them to think and discuss these questions with their classmates, whether it is in pairs, groups, or the entire classroom.
3. As the students discuss and give you answers to your questions, write this information on the board so they can take notes and also reference it during their writing time.

The outline is brief and you, as the teacher, can develop your own method that follows this outline. Teachers must be just as creative as their students when developing material and presenting it to their students. Engage them with visual stimulation and questions. If your students feel comfortable and confident about the details of a subject, writing will come more naturally.

Some other great questions to include during a warm-up discussion about the Golden Gate Bridge are:

1. What are some adjectives you can use to describe the Golden Gate Bridge?
2. How can you describe the area around the bridge?
3. What do you see on the bridge and why?
4. What information would you like to know about this bridge if you visited it?

Warm Up Outline

Another aspect to writing that some of us may remember from our own beginning writing days is the outline of our writing. This is just as important as the words, sentences, and paragraphs themselves. Giving your students a good structure to follow in their writing will make their task much easier since they already have so much to worry about in consideration to writing in a whole different language than their own. A good structure can help them develop a quality writing piece and it will build their confidence since they already have a strategic template to guide them. We previously discussed paragraph structure in this chapter and your students can apply that structure right to their writing task outline.

They know that each paragraph needs a topic sentence and supporting sentences, usually following. A good way to explain the writing task outline is to start with the paragraph structure and expand it to the different paragraphs in the complete writing exercise. Almost all writing has the basic structure of introduction, three supporting paragraphs, and a conclusion. The trick here, is to show your students how to craft their introduction paragraphs to give their reader an overview of what the body of writing will be about. This can be a great way to warm them up for the writing exercise while also giving them another exceptional tool to writing in English.

Here is an example outline for a general writing exercise:

✓ **Introduction Paragraph**
1. Topic sentence that covers the main topic of the writing work.
2. Supporting sentence that covers the topic of the first paragraph.
3. Supporting sentence that covers the topic of the second paragraph.
4. Supporting sentence that covers the topic of the third paragraph.

✓ **Paragraph One**
1. Topic sentence for the paragraph.
2. Supporting sentence.

3. Supporting sentence.

4. Supporting sentence.

✓ **Paragraph Two**

1. Topic sentence for the paragraph.

2. Supporting sentence.

3. Supporting sentence.

4. Supporting sentence.

✓ **Paragraph Three**

1. Topic sentence for the paragraph.

2. Supporting sentence.

3. Supporting sentence.

4. Supporting sentence.

✓ **Conclusion Paragraph**

1. Topic sentence that summarizes the main topic of the writing work.

2. Supporting sentence.

3. Supporting sentence.

4. Supporting sentence.

There are many different types of writing tasks you can assign to your students and not all will have a simple structure like the example above. You will have to develop an outline warm-up exercise that will fit your specific lesson material. Remember to give excellent examples, visuals, and engage your students in discussion surrounding any warm-up activity.

Timing Student Writing

After your students are all warmed-up and ready to put their pens to paper, it is important to remember that keeping a controlled environment for learning not only benefits the teacher, but also the students. If you finished the warm-up with success, you cannot just tell your students to begin writing. It is important to keep control and guide them on their writing task. Set timing for their writing, allowing them to approach their writing tasks in an organized and well thought out way. Your students should have a good idea about the topic they are writing about and they have discussed it with you and their classmates. They should also have the basic understanding of how to develop an entire piece of writing since you gave them a great outline example. Next is to set the timing for them to develop their drafts.

During the drafting period, your students will take the information they know about the topic and put it in the outline format. You can even give them some writing outline templates to reference as well as having it on the board for them to reference. After they have developed their drafts, you set the timing for them to actually piece it all together on a separate paper in the medium draft stage. Sometimes this can be the final draft, depending on how they feel about the final draft checklist questions they will answer after developing their medium draft.

Here is a great timing outline for writing.

1. Developing a draft and filling in their outline templates with the information they have attained in the warm-up exercise.
2. They transfer their outline structure to a blank sheet of paper, developing their medium draft or final draft ready to compare it to the writing checklist.
3. They compare their writing work with the writing checklist and make sure they have a well-developed paper. If they need to make adjustments, they can develop a final draft from their medium draft.
4. Students will develop their final drafts and this time could also be a good opportunity for group or pair discussion and review as they share their work with others.

Here are some example questions for the writing checklist.

✓ Is my grammar and spelling correct?

✓ Is my punctuation correct?

✓ Did I use the write format for this writing assignment?

✓ Do I have an introduction and conclusion?

✓ Did I clearly cover the main topic?

Writing can be a fun and fulfilling lesson for your students and if you are prepared and have thoroughly thought out your material and presentation, your students should be successful. A good lesson plan is essential, like with all English subjects you will teach to your students, being a prepared teacher will allow you and your students to have mutual success completing lesson aims and objectives. There are many different writing exercises you can give your students and they can all be adapted to any student level and/or age. Remember, relevancy is important so know your students. Reviews, advertisements, articles, emails, letters, instructions, memos, applications, resumes, reports, and stories are just a few excellent tasks for writing lessons.

Creative Teacher Thinking

Starting with writing warm-ups, develop a lesson plan that will have your students write an advertisement for the Golden Gate Bridge in

San Francisco, California. How would you present the material and set the timing for their writing?

Chapter Fourteen

Pronunciation Development and Instruction

Chapter Overview:

Pronunciation Importance

Is There an Echo in Here?

Syllable and Word Stress

Intonation Focus

Pronunciation Importance

The world of English learning is often mysterious and unique since some English learners will study English for decades and have little communication skills and incorrect pronunciation. Even in parts of Europe where English is the native language, different accents can blur a word to an incomprehensible sound. Some study grammar and can complete Intermediate English textbooks with ease, but when they travel to an English speaking country, no one can understand the words that they worked so hard to learn. This is where pronunciation comes in and it is a very important aspect of teaching English as a foreign language.

Is There An Echo In Here?

One great way of teaching your students the correct pronunciation of a word is to have them repeat the way you pronounce the word. Yes, this may often seem like a boring exercise for them and you to do, but with a little creativity you can make it fun with them learning new pronunciation quickly. When introducing new vocabulary, you should first say the word so they can hear the correct way to pronounce it before you ask them to repeat the word. This will engrain the correct way to pronounce the word without them making up sounds that they think may be correct. In some instances, students will stumble upon a word naturally that they have trouble pronouncing, so always keep an ear out for those moments. It is important to cut out bad habits before they grow.

When you are teaching pronunciation using a repeat method, you can utilize the whole class, separate students into groups, or practice pronunciation individually. Imagine each student as a separate musical instrument as they repeat new words aloud. You will use your body language to raise tone or have them put emphasis in the words they are yelling out. Pronunciation as a class can make pronunciation more fun and allow the shy students to participate without feeling embarrassed about their speaking ability.

On an individual basis, you can begin with class repetition and then move to individual students throughout the room. For example, you would begin with the class, having them repeat the word several times saying "class," and then "Mary," queuing Mary to repeat the word solo. This can be fun and you can also use your non-verbal communication and movements to get a few laughs from your students.

Creative Teacher Thinking

Why is your student's ability to pronounce words correct important? Can you assume that intermediate students will have correct pronunciation? How would you combine a class pronunciation repeating exercise with an individual repeating exercise?

Syllable and Word Stress

In the English language we use a lot of stress on our syllables and words. Where we place the stress in a word can often alter the pronunciation and may cause confusion on the face of the person you are saying the word to. This is why you need to teach your students the correct areas to stress in a word, or the word itself in order for them to have correct pronunciation and effective communication. You can break pronunciation words into syllables and show them where the stress is in the word. You can also show them the words you stress in a sentence in order to give those words more meaning, also showing them how English is a harmonious type of language because of the different stress we put on different words.

Here is an example of stressing a syllable in a word and how you can show your students in an example:

1. Our pronunciation word is **TA**ble. Please repeat after me. **TA**ble.
2. Where do we put the stress in our word **TA**ble?
3. We put the stress on the **TA** in **TA**ble.

Here is an example of stressing a word in a sentence and how you can show your students in an example:

1. We want to go. Which words would we stress in this sentence?
2. We would stress the word **WANT** and the word **GO**.
3. We **WANT** to **GO**. Repeat after me, we **WANT** to **GO**.
4. Why do we stress the words **WANT** and **GO**?
5. We stress these words in the sentence because they are more important words than the others.

It is a good idea to always remember to mark the words and syllables that are stressed in new vocabulary and in the example sentences you may use those stress words in. This will allow your students to get more comfortable with using stress and they will begin to understand it more and in most cases, naturally develop the correct stress in syllables and words in sentences over time.

Creative Teacher Thinking

Why is teaching stress on words important? How would you develop a vocabulary list of 5 new words and show the different syllable stress areas?

Intonation Focus

Having a good understanding of intonation will give your students a voice and the power to control what they say and the meaning behind it with just a simple change in tone. When your students understand intonation, you will give them the ability to develop their English voice. We discussed English voice and tone when reading in Chapter Twelve and those values will carry to your student's pronunciation and speech. Teaching your students correct intonation will also allow them to express emotion and change the meaning of sentences with a simple fluctuation of tone. When someone is sad, they have a specific tone and the same goes for when they are happy, excited, or interested in something or someone.

Here is a great example of intonation when it is applied to a few sentences:

1. You found your keys? This intonation is a question tone and it emphasizes the sentence as a question.
2. I did! The response will be an intonation of joy and relief.

Changing voice tone, up or down, can add that intonation and change meanings, so it is important to have a lot of practice with this when giving a lesson on intonation and allowing your students to build confidence as they find their English voice. A fun exercise for intonation that will engage the whole class is to pick a drama script with many types of intonations and tonal fluctuations. It will be a great way to encourage communication as they practice their lines and will keep them engaged in the lesson material.

Creative Teacher Thinking

What will teaching intonation provide to your students? Why is intonation important and what would be a few fun activities for your students to do to learn intonation?

Chapter Fifteen

Practical Discussion and Communication

Chapter Overview:

Open Communication

Discussion Warm Ups

Communicative Activities

Keeping It Going

Expanding Conversation

When Teaching Discussion

Quality Structure

Be Engaged

Open Communication

In the beginning of this book we discussed knowing your student's English goals and we noted that all English learners, regardless of level and age, want to be able to communicate in English and express their feeling and thoughts. No one wants to learn a language to never use it in a practical situation and since English has become somewhat of a global language, English teachers must focus on teaching their students how to communicate and discuss topics with other English speakers effectively.

From the beginning of your class, you can open the communication gates and allow your students to begin basic communication from the get go. Encouraging a line of open communication between students and student to teacher is an excellent strategy, when you are not presenting new material of course. A great way of setting the standard for conversation in class is to let students participate with one another about daily topics. Think about your previous and/or current jobs. You may find yourself shuffling into the office after a relaxing weekend and sparking up routine conversation with colleagues. How was your evening? How was your weekend? Did you do anything special? These are all excellent questions you can provide your students with as they ask and answer the questions in pairs before getting the presentation going. It is not only what native speakers do and say, it gets them thinking and communicating in English in a guided way.

Creative Teacher Thinking

How important is encouraging communication and discussion in your class? Why? What are some strategies for allowing your students to have open conversation with each other?

Discussion Warm Ups

You may be noticing warm ups as a trend in our effective teaching chapters. Just as in writing, reading, and pronunciation lessons, warming up before practical discussion and communication exercises is important. Remember, your students, in most cases, are coming from home, work, and/or school where they speak exclusively in their native language. Transitioning from thinking, speaking, and comprehending in their native language to English can be difficult and possibly frustrating at certain student levels. They may also be thinking about personal matters that can distract them in class, so get them warmed up and back into the full English swing of things before going into presentation and practice.

Here are a few excellent warm up activities you can use in your lessons:

Current Events: Current events are a great way to get your student's English minds flowing in the right direction. Your material may vary depending on the age, professions, interests, and levels of your students, so always be thinking relevancy when preparing your current event warm up material. For older, business professionals, you can use world and local events to spark that much needed English conversation. For younger students, sports, movies, cartoons, television series, and social media make for good content. Discussing current events is also a great way to get your students to begin expressing their thoughts and feelings about certain subjects and will help build confidence and English skill.

Letter Game: The letter game is another excellent warm up and can be fun for your younger students and lower level students that may not fully comprehend a current issue. The letter game uses some existing English vocabulary to help your students think and speak in English. For example, you could start the warmup up with the word dog and write that word on the board for your students to reference. After, you will choose a student and they must say a word that begins with the last letter of the word the previous person used. In our example, dog ends with G, so the next student will say a word starting with G, like good. This will involve the whole class as they work their way around the room listening, speaking, and thinking in English.

Communicative Activities

Communicative activities are an excellent way to guide your students in discussion and allow them to navigate questions without needing to think too hard about a creative expression. Communicative activities are very popular in ESL and can be very effective in building real life English skills. In communicative activities, the material is set up in a particular way to inhibit quick and useful questions and responses. You can create a worksheet for each student in their pair teams with guided material. One student will have the answers and the other student will have the questions. It is important to make these types of exercises relevant to real life and practical to ensure your students will have the correct language when using their skills in a real situation.

Ordering from a menu and addressing your server is an important part of everyday life, especially for your students, who will often use their English outside of their home country, traveling. For example, print a restaurant menu off the internet and provide each student with a copy. Student A will be the customer and Student B will be the waiter or waitress. Before letting your students begin the communicative activity on their own, give detailed examples on how they should create their questions and answers as they order and discuss the menu with one another. Examples are the key to success in this exercise and you could even show them how it's done in the presentation before letting them loose in their practice exercise.

Creative Teacher Thinking

What is a good warm up activity and why is it important to have before beginning the lesson material? How could you combine a warm up exercise with a communicative activity with a smooth transition?

Keeping It Going

Once you have established a routine communication amongst your students, give them the skills to keep those conversations going. After your students have begun to elicit a conversation, asking and answering questions, they will be excited and ready to give their discussions a more natural flow. In practice, they have only used scripted discussion tools and this is a good beginning, but not natural. They will need to know how to engage further with questions which extend conversations and show interest for what their discussion partner is saying. There is also an aspect of non-verbal communication, using our body language to show interest and that they are listening effectively.

Here are some great examples of questions that will help your students extend their conversations further:

- ✓ What is that?
- ✓ What do you think about that?
- ✓ How about you?
- ✓ What is that like?

✓ Do you enjoy it?

Here are some great examples for using body language in a conversation:

✓ Look your speaking partner in the eyes.
✓ Smile when appropriate (if not a serious conversation).
✓ Nod in agreement throughout the conversation.
✓ Try not to cross arms, lean back, and/or have things in the way of you and your speaking partner.
✓ Face your body toward your speaking partner.

We can also use key words to show interest:

✓ Really?
✓ No way!
✓ Awesome!
✓ Cool.
✓ That's great.
✓ That's so interesting.

Expanding Conversations

Your students have had a lot of speaking and discussion practice at this point and now you can turn the discussion up a notch and let them expand on the conversation more. You may have been guiding the conversations thus far and now you can give them a bit of freedom to get creative. When teaching your students how to expand on their conversations, giving examples and writing them on the board or passing out a worksheet will be very beneficial in their success. Some great exercises for expanding discussions are debates, interview questions, outlining likes and dislikes, as well as role-playing. Another great way to expand conversations is to create an opinion about something and sharing those opinions with their partners. Like a debate, it will allow your students to engage in conversation that is more natural and relatable to everyday situations.

Here are a few phrases for your students to assert opinions into their discussions:

- ✓ I (don't) believe.
- ✓ I (don't) think.
- ✓ In my opinion.
- ✓ I agree, because.

✓ I disagree, because.

There are many different ways to approach discussion expansion, but it's always important to remember to make sure your student's discussion skill set is present and up to par before going too far into speaking and discussion expansion.

Creative Teacher Thinking

What are some great ways to keep a discussion going and how can you present this to your students? Why is it important to give your students the knowledge they need to keep a conversation moving and expanding the discussion as well? What are some great phrases used to insert opinions, agreements and disagreements?

When Teaching Discussion

There are a few hallmarks to consider when teaching discussion and letting your students create their very own discussions in the production stage of speaking and discussion lessons. As discussed before, keeping things relevant and interesting to your students while giving them the knowledge they need is paramount. Learners of English are not going to want to discuss anything that they normally wouldn't care to discuss in their daily lives in their native language. Thinking about topics for your discussion lessons can be easy and fun, but always remember to do the self-test first. Ask yourself a few questions to ensure you are on the right track with your material.

Here are some great questions to keep your material relevant and interesting:

- ✓ How would I feel about discussing this topic?
- ✓ Is this relevant to my student's age, level, and interests?
- ✓ Will this topic evoke enough discussion?
- ✓ Can my students expand and formulate opinions about the topic?
- ✓ Is this material appropriate culturally?

Quality Structure

Structure is another important aspect of discussion lessons, so keep in mind the lesson plan format and PPP outline that you will use during the course of your ESL career. Don't let things linger for too long. If a specific exercise takes too long, students will lose interest and will shut down or revert to their native language to spice up their classroom exercise. That being said, too short of a time period for an exercise can leave students frustrated if they didn't fully grasp the material before moving to the next exercise. Make sure to keep your timetable in order and keep your students engaged and interested in the material.

Be Engaged

Just as important as timing, keep your ears open and move around the classroom to ensure all students are still on the main topic for that specific exercise. During your student's discussions, especially during the production stage, maintain a presence even though they are engaged in their own personal conversations that don't include you. Being an engaged teacher during discussion exercises will help you maintain topic control, ensure that English is the only language being spoken, and also alert you to any individual student problems you may need to address to get them back on track and having an effective discussion with their partner.

Discussion Lesson Checklist

- ✓ Is my lesson plan amazing?
- ✓ Is my lesson material relevant and interesting?
- ✓ Did I make time for a warm up exercise?
- ✓ Does my presentation explain the material and the expectations of the discussion well?

✓ Is my practice exercise relevant and contain communicative activities, keeping a discussion going and have an element of expansion?

✓ Is my lesson structured and does it have a time element?

✓ How will I engage my students and keep an eye out during practice and production?

Creative Teacher Thinking

What are a few important elements to remember when conducting your discussion lesson? Outline an hour speaking and discussion lesson from the start of class to the end.

Chapter Sixteen

Listening Lessons

Chapter Overview:

Why Listening?

Listening Lesson Structure

Listening Lesson Material

Aspects of Listening

Why Listening?

There is a 99% chance that every single one of your students wants to learn English in order to communicate in English effectively, to speak and express their feeling naturally in another language. Speaking is one of the most important aspects of learning English, or any language, but how can you speak if you can't understand the questions and long winded sentences being thrown at you in a discussion. This is why listening is extremely important to teach your students and teach it effectively.

The good news is that from day one and possibly before even walking into your classroom, they have begun listening to English in some form. In most cases, your students are exposed to English through music, television series, and movies. Unfortunately, they may know a song's music and will be able to identify and tell you who sings it, but they won't know or understand the lyrics. You can build on this and they will most surely begin listening to you speak the first day of class and will entrust you to lead them to the path of listening comprehension.

Lesson Structure

When structuring your listening lesson, ask yourself how you would like to learn to listen to another language. Some of you may have an interest in other cultures and languages since you are learning how to teach English to non-native speakers and will normally travel to new and exciting countries to do so. Get your students engaged in listening before you start with presentation and practice. Let them get comfortable with listening to English by using a warm up exercise that may or may not be related to the main topic you will introduce later. Warm ups may be sounding redundant, but it truly is a helpful way to get your students relaxed and moving in the right direction for your listening exercise. Spending a little time on a game or activity is a great idea. You can even use this in conjunction with discussion.

After a fun warm up, present the topic for their listening lesson and introduce some important information on the subject. Let them pair up or get in groups to discuss and get to know the subject that will be in the listening portion of the lesson. Outline a set of questions before playing or even reading what they will listen to. When they have a good idea of what the questions will be, they will be more motivated to pick out the answers when listening. After the listening portion, let them share and discuss their answers with their classmates and you. This is a good opportunity for you to also address any issues that are reoccurring in more than two students.

You will repeat this exercise using the same audio as before with new information and questions about the topic; however, it should contain more difficult content and be followed by more difficult questions for discussion. When the listening comprehension is complete, open the floor to a more expanded discussion on the topic, but remember that this part of the lesson should be no longer than the second listening activity. This structure will give your students ample discussion time about the topic and they can get a better understanding of their listening ability, as well as you.

Listening Comprehension Outline:

1. Ask yourself how you would like the material for the lesson if you were the student.
2. Listening warm up.
3. Present the subject of what they will be listening to and let them see the listening comprehension questions for discussion.
4. Introduce the first listening activity.
5. Allow time for discussion and comparing answers on the first listening activity.
6. Introduce the more challenging listening activity.
7. Allow time for discussion and comparing answers on the second listening activity.
8. Create a follow up and discussion period regarding the lesson and listening activities.

Creative Teacher Thinking

Why is listening important to teach your students? Is it only applicable for a specific English level or age? What are the main elements to your listening comprehension lesson? Should your listening material be relevant?

Listening Lesson Material

When searching for your listening comprehension material, you may find many options, but it is important to decide what the best fit is for your students. You need to take a good look into what types of situations your students may face in real life situations when they will need their English skills. There are many different ways to implement listening material and all have their own positive and negative attributes, so think like your students when choosing and developing your listening lesson.

You could use the audio that comes with the various English textbooks and these are all great when it comes to structure. Your students can follow along in the textbook or have a reference point to relate the audio to. On the other hand, audio recordings from textbooks are often one size fits all and in some cases very generic. Another choice is your own voice, but then again, your students are already familiar and quite comfortable with the sound of your voice and how you structure your speech. Your voice could be a good starting point for some students, but challenging them and introducing them to different voices is sometimes a better choice. Videos from the internet and other audio clips that are accompanied with video are also great choices and can show the students the importance in non-verbal communication as well.

You want to ease your students into listening activities and structure is great, but at the end of the day, your students will be out in the real world, in real life English speaking situations. You want to make your listening material authentic and relatable to the real life situations they will soon face. Use material that will show them how native English speakers speak, move, use non-verbal communication, phrasal verbs, idioms, slang, and all the intricate parts of communicating in English.

Creative Teacher Thinking

What types of audio clips or videos that would be useful to use during your listening lessons? What are the advantages and disadvantages of using textbook audios? What is the main purpose for your students to learn great listening skills?

Aspects of Listening

The key aspects behind the listening comprehension exercise that uses the same audio recording, is that the student will hear it once and answer the questions while understanding the main idea and content of the audio clip. The second time they listen will focus on listening for details and other more specific areas of the conversation. This creates challenge and will help your student remain focused on specific areas each time they listen to the audio.

The structure of this type of listening lesson is all about guided discovery while listening to the audio. First time around they will be thinking about those questions and short examples you gave them which are focused on main ideas in the audio. The second time, they will have already understood the main idea and will have the questions and short examples of the more detailed stuff they should be listening for.

Here is an excellent example of a short audio script and the questions that will accompany the separate times they listen to it:

Audio script of Tom and Maria's conversation:

Tom: Hey Maria, have you found the Smith file yet?

Maria: Sorry Tom, it's still missing. When is the meeting?

Tom: The meeting is Today at 3:30 pm and I need to find that file.

Maria: Ok, I will keep searching.

Tom: Thanks Maria, I will come back this afternoon before the meeting.

Questions relating to the general topic of the audio:

1. Where do you think Tom and Maria are?
2. How many speakers are there in the audio?
3. What is the main problem?

Questions relating to the details of the audio:

1. What is the name of the file they are looking for?
2. When do they need to find it?
3. What time is Tom coming back to see Maria?

You can see how different the questions are in relation to the general topic and the details surrounding the topic of the conversation. This is a good format to use when developing your listening questions. You can also introduce vocabulary before the listening activity to give students a little better idea of what is being discussed. The detailed questions allow your students to really think about what is happening in the conversation and get a better feeling to the condition of the scenario. Remember to introduce the task before each time they listen to the audio so they have a good idea of what they need to be listening for.

There are many different listening activities you can use to develop your student's listening skills. Here are a few great examples:

- ✓ Following directions on a map with audio.
- ✓ Use classical stories that are easy to follow.
- ✓ Songs in English are always a great choice.
- ✓ Teacher reading.
- ✓ Comparing an audio clip with a picture.
- ✓ Creating a timetable of events using the audio.

Creative Teacher Thinking

Develop a listening comprehension lesson using a piece of material you have found on your own. How will you develop this lesson and what are the different parts you will need to include? Can you think of any listening activities that were not discussed or listed?

Chapter Seventeen

Get to Know Grammar

Chapter Overview:

Grammar Basics

Nouns, Verbs, and Subjects

The Many Verb Forms

Using Prepositions

Using Articles

The Adjective Spice

Grammar Basics

The words we use for things, people and places are combined with action words, giving our language life and expression. When you are teaching grammar to your students, you need to have a good understanding of basic grammar aspects that are used commonly and often. The following chapter will list some of the most important grammar areas that you as an English language teacher should get to know fairly well. You will soon enter the world of ESL teachers and should already have a good knowledge of grammar, so here is some reference material for you to look at and think about as you develop your grammar lesson plans.

Nouns, Verbs, and Subjects

- ✓ **Nouns** are used to designate names to people, things, and places. Example: House, Hospital, Martin.
- ✓ **Verbs** are our action words and help us give animation to our sentences. Verbs can also be used to describe a state of being as well. Example: Running, writing, calling.
- ✓ **Subjects** tell us what our sentences are about. They are also used to tell us what someone is doing as well. Example: **Martin** enjoys exercise.
- ✓ **Subject Pronouns** are used when you don't use the specific name of a person or thing. Example: **He** enjoys exercise.

The Many Verb Forms

As mentioned, verbs are the action words in English and give our sentences animation. Verbs are often tricky for English students because verbs can take on many different forms. These forms are important to understand so you can effectively teach them to your students.

✓ **The Infinitive Verb Form** is the original version of the verb and is the most widely known by your students. Example: To run.

✓ **The Gerund Verb Form** is the (ing) addition to the verb. Example: Running

✓ **The Past Simple Verb Form** is the verb in the past simple tense and can be noted by the (ed) added to the verb. In some cases, the past simple tense will also change the verbs spelling. These verbs are called irregular verbs. Example: Walk - Walked. Run - Ran (irregular verb).

✓ **The Past Participle Verb Form** is used when the sentence is passive. This will change the verb and add an (n) to the end of the verb or in some cases in the middle of the word. Example: See - Seen.

✓ **Auxiliary Verbs** are a pair of verbs used together to add meaning to a verb that may not have any meaning if it were alone in a sentence. Example: I (am working). They (are running).

✓ **Irregular Verbs** are verbs that change in spelling and pronunciation when used in the past simple tense form. Example: Run - Ran. Swim - Swam.

Using Prepositions

There are many different ways to use prepositions and this may also be confusing for some of your students. Prepositions come in all different sizes and shapes, so covering each specific type of preposition in their designated groups will help clear up some of the confusion. There are prepositions of time, place, direction, amount, manner, and cause. Grouping them together will make it easier for your students to realize the type of situation being discussed, maybe time or place. Some languages use prepositions differently, so make sure to give excellent attention to prepositions and their correct usage.

✓ Prepositions of Time (**soon, before**).
✓ Prepositions of Place (**in front of, behind**).

Using Articles

For your students, articles are those annoying words that they can't quite figure out how to use in the correct place and in the correct situation. Taking time to explain articles and how they are used will save you a lot of time and energy later, so remember to fit this into your syllabus if you know your students are in need of some article time.

Articles come before nouns and have specific attributes to contribute to a sentence:

✓ **Article (A)** is an indefinite article and is used to introduce a noun, add a singular aspect, and also describe a general noun. Example: A tree fell in the forest yesterday. This introduces the tree in a general way.

✓ **Article (An)** is an indefinite article that is used before nouns beginning with a vowel. Example: An elephant is in the street. The (An) is used before the vowel (e) in elephant.

✓ **Article (The)** is a definite article and is used for specific nouns. It is also used for nouns that have already been introduced in the sentence or story using the article (A or An). Example: An elephant is in the street. The elephant is dirty.

There are many rules regarding English articles and the above is only the basic rules behind their use. As an English teacher, expand your grammar knowledge that may have been diminished since our elementary grammar days.

The Adjective Spice

Verbs give us our sentences action and adjectives give our sentences spice. Imagine English without adjectives and this will give you a good reason to stress the importance of knowing adjectives to your students. Your students will enjoy learning adjectives, because these are the words that will help them express themselves in a deeper way.

There are many different types of adjectives, but they generally come in three different ways:

- ✓ Identifying
- ✓ Quantifying
- ✓ Describing

Describing adjectives include shape, color, material, opinions, comparative forms, and superlative forms. There are more, so it is a good idea to look into different types of adjectives used for describing words a bit more in detail. Identifying adjectives are used to describe ownership of a specific noun. A few identifying adjectives include my, his, hers, theirs, ours, these, that, and so on. Other adjectives will define how many there is of something. A few quantifying adjectives include, some, many, all, both, every, neither and so on.

There are also rules relating to the order of things when it comes to using multiple adjectives in one sentence. Your students will begin using adjectives for every word they come across and this can have its own problems if they do not know how to order their adjectives in a sentence correctly. When they understand the order of adjectives, they will be able to formulate perfect descriptive sentences that sound natural.

Here is the order of adjectives:

1. Ownership/whose.
2. How many of something.
3. Opinion on the subject.
4. Size and shape.
5. Age
6. Color
7. Origin

8. Material

9. Use

Knowing grammar very well will help you successfully introduce it to your students in a way they will be able to fully understand, leading to more confidence as they continue to blossom into exceptional English communicators. When developing your grammar lesson plan, make sure to do a little homework and put together a grammar lesson that is informative and easy for your students to understand.

Conclusion

The Easy TEFL Guide to Teaching English as a Foreign Language is an essential book for anyone who is interested in gaining knowledge to become a certified TEFL teacher. The content in this book allows you to obtain important understanding on the key aspects that surround planning and developing quality lesson plans and the skills needed to implement your lesson plan in class. Remember to plan for success and keep things relevant to allow for maximum confidence building and communication amongst your students. Teaching English as a Foreign Language is a rewarding career that will enlighten you to new and interesting cultures around the world. It may be just what you are looking for in your life or something you want to do for a short period of time, regardless of your commitment, you will see the spark and enthusiasm in your students and that will last a lifetime. Enjoy teaching English while fulfilling the dreams and goals of your students, as well as your own.

Made in the USA
Las Vegas, NV
14 March 2021